THE STRUCTURE

OF

MAGIC

II

By
JOHN GRINDER
and
RICHARD BANDLER

Science and Behavior Books, Inc.
Palo Alto, California 94306

Library of Congress Card Number 75-12452
ISBN 08314-0049-8

Cover by Josh Doolan

To

Leslie Cameron

one of the world's most creative

family therapists

and to

Steve Gilligan

one of the world's most effective

hypnotists

with

our deepest respect

Table Of Contents

PART I
Representational Systems — Other Maps For The
Same Territory 1

PART II
Incongruity 27

PART III
Fuzzy Functions 97

PART IV
Family Therapy — The Delicate Flower 123

PART V
Formal Notation 163

Epilogue 195

Bibliography 197

PART I

Representational Systems –
Other Maps For
The Same Territory

INTRODUCTION

In Volume One of *The Structure of Magic* we began the process of making the magical skills of potent psychotherapists available to other practitioners in a learnable and explicit form. We presented to you the intuitions these psychotherapeutic wizards have about language in a step-by-step form so that you could train yourself to use your own intuitions, thereby increasing your skill. In this second volume, we intend to present more of the intuitions these wizards have about language, and to extend our work to include the intuitions and systematic behavior of these wizards relative to other ways a human being can both represent and communicate his world. While you read this volume, we would like you to keep in mind several aspects of *The Structure of Magic I.*

Human beings live in a "real world." We do not, however, operate directly or immediately upon that world, but, rather, we operate within that world using a map or a series of maps of that world to guide our behavior within it. These maps, or representational systems, necessarily differ from the territory that they model by the three universal processes of human modeling: *Generalization, Deletion,* and *Distortion.* When people come to us in therapy expressing pain and dissatisfaction, the limitations which they experience are, typically, in their *representation* of the world and not in the world itself.

The most thoroughly studied and best understood of the representational systems of human modeling maps is that of human language. The most explicit and complete model of natural language is transformational grammar. Transformational grammar is, therefore, a Meta-model — a representation of the structure of human language — itself a representation of the world of experience.

Human language systems are, themselves, derived representations of a more complete model — the sum total of the experience the particular human being has had in his life. Transformational linguists have developed a number of concepts and mechanisms to describe how the way that people speak — their Surface Structures — is actually derived from their full linguistic representation — the Deep Structures. The transformational Meta-models describe these concepts and mechanisms explicitly — they are specific cases of the general modeling processes of Generalization, Distortion and Deletion.

In adapting the concepts and mechanisms of the transformational model of the human representational system of language for the purposes of therapy, we developed a formal Meta-model for therapy. This formal Meta-model is:

    (a) *Explicit* — that is, it describes the process of therapy in a step-by-step manner, guaranteeing that the Meta-model is learnable; this results in an explicit strategy for therapy.

    (b) *Independent of content* — dealing with the form of the process and, therefore, having universal applicability.

The Meta-model relies only upon the intuitions which every native speaker has of his language. The overall implication of the Meta-model for therapy is the assumption of *well-formed in therapy*. Well-formed in therapy is a set of conditions which the Surface Structures the client uses in therapy must meet in order to be acceptable. Using this appropriate grammar for therapy, we, as therapists, can assist our clients in expanding the portions of their representations which impoverish and limit them. This results in enriching their lives in such a way that they experience more options in their behavior, more opportunities to experience the joys and richness that life has to offer. When integrated with the people-helper skills which you, as a therapist, already have available to you, this process of growth and change is profoundly accelerated. This language of growth, then, is truly an essential part of *The Structure of Magic*.

THE MAP IS NOT THE TERRITORY

One of the important conclusions we established in *Magic I* is that the map necessarily differs from the territory it is representing, and that each map will differ from every other map in some way. The map or model that we have been referring to so far is a simplification of a more complex process. In fact, the map we have been referring to is actually a series of maps which result when we model our experiences by using what we call *representational systems*.

INPUT CHANNELS

There are three major *input channels* by which we, as human beings, receive information about the world around us — *vision*, *audition*, and *kinesthetics* (body sensations). (The remaining two most commonly accepted sensory input channels — smell and taste — are, apparently, little utilized as ways of gaining information about the world.)[1] Each of these three sensory input channels provides us with an ongoing stream of information which we use to organize our experience. Within each of these input channels, there are a number of specialized receptors which carry specific kinds of information. For example, neurophysiologists have distinguished chromatic (color) receptors within the eye — the cones located in the center or fovea of the eye — from the chromatic (non-color) receptors — the rods located in the periphery of the eye. Again, in the kinesthetic input channel, specialized receptors for pressure, temperature, pain and deep senses (proprioceptors) have been shown to exist. The number of distinctions in each of the input channels is not limited by the number of specialized receptors in each of these channels. Combinations or recurring patterns of stimulation of one or more of these specialized receptors in each of the sensory channels provide information of a more complex nature. For example, the common experience of wetness can be broken down into a combination of several of the kinesthetically different, specialized receptors within the major receptors. Furthermore, the input channels may combine to provide information of an even more complex nature. For example, we receive the experience of texture through a combination of visual, kinesthetic and (in some cases) auditory stimulations.

For our purposes at this point, we need only point out that information received through one of the input channels may be stored or represented in a map or model which is different from that channel. Perhaps the most frequently occurring example of this is the ability that each of us has to represent visual information, say, in the form of *natural language* — that is, words, phrases, and sentences of our language. Probably as frequent, but not usually consciously recognized, is our ability to make pictures or images out of the information we receive through the auditory channel. As I sit here typing this sentence, I hear the crackling and hissing sound of logs burning in the fireplace behind me. Using this auditory information as input, I create the image of the logs burning. Thus, I create a visual representation from auditory input. If, at this point, you, the reader, were to pause and allow yourself to become aware of the sounds around you without shifting the focus of your eyes, you would find yourself able to create visual images for many of the sounds you detected. This ability to create representations of input from one input channel based upon information coming from another channel will be the topic of discussion later in this volume.

REPRESENTATIONAL SYSTEMS

Each of us, as a human being, has available a number of different ways of representing our experience of the world. Following are some examples of the representational systems each of us can use to represent our experiences.

We have five recognized senses for making contact with the world — we *see*, we *hear*, we *feel*, we *taste* and we *smell*. In addition to these sensory systems, we have a language system which we use to represent our experience. We may store our experience directly in the representational system most closely associated with that sensory channel. We may choose to close our eyes and create a visual image of a red square shifting to green and then to blue, or a spiral wheel of silver and black slowly revolving counter-clockwise, or the image of some person we know well. Or, we may choose to close our eyes (or not) and to create a kinesthetic representation (a body sensation, a feeling), placing our hands against a wall and pushing as hard as we can, feeling the tightening of the muscles in our arms and shoulders, becoming aware of the texture of the floor beneath our feet. Or, we may choose to become aware of the prickling sensation of the heat of the flames of a fire burning, or of sensing the pressure of several light blankets covering our sighing bodies as we sink softly into our beds. Or we may choose to close our eyes (or not) and create an auditory (sound) representation — the patter of tinkling raindrops, the crack of distant thunder and its following roll through the once-silent hills, the squeal of singing tires on a quiet country road, or the blast of a taxi horn through the deafening roars of a noisy city. Or we may close our eyes and create a gustatory (taste) representation of the sour flavor of a lemon, or the sweetness of honey, or the saltiness of a stale potato chip. Or we may choose to close our eyes (or not) and create an olfactory (smell) representation of a fragrant rose, or rancid milk, or the pungent aroma of cheap perfume.

Some of you may have noticed that, while reading through the descriptions of the above paragraph, you actually experienced seeing a particular color or movement; feeling hardness, warmth, or roughness; hearing a specific sound; experiencing certain tastes or smells. You may have experienced all or only some of these sensations. Some of them were more detailed and immediate for you than others. For some of the descriptions you may have had no experience at all. These differences in your experiences are exactly what we are describing. Those of you who had a sharp, clear *picture* of some experience have a rich, highly developed, visual representational system. Those of you who were able to develop a strong *feeling* of weight, temperature, or texture have a refined, highly developed kinesthetic representational system. And so on with the other possible ways associated with our five senses that we, as humans, have of representing our experiences.

Notice that the description in the last paragraph is missing something. Specifically, each of the descriptions in the paragraph before it about visual, kinesthetic, auditory, gustatory and olfactory experiences was not represented in those specific sensory systems, but rather in an altogether different system — a language system — the *digital* representational system. We described with words, phrases and sentences the experiences in the different representational systems. We selected these words carefully — for example, if we want to describe something in a visual representational system, we select words such as:

black . . . clear . . . spiral . . . image

If we want to describe something in an auditory system, we select words such as:

tinkling . . . silent . . . squeal . . . blast

This sentence is an example of the way that we represent our experience in the language. This ability which we have to represent our experiences in each of our different representational systems with words — that is, in the digital system — identifies one of the most useful characteristics of language representational systems — their universality. That is to say, by using our language representational systems, we are able to present our experience of any of the other representational systems. Since this is true, we refer to our language system as the *digital* system. We can use it to create a map of our world. When we use the sentence:

He showed me some vivid images.

we are creating a *language* map of our *visual* map of some experience which we have had. We may choose to create a language representation by combining different representational systems. When we use the sentence:

She reeled backwards, tripping over the screaming animal writhing with pain from bitter smoke choking the sunlight out.

we are using a language representation which presupposes a series of maps of our experience, at least one from each of these five representational systems.

For example:

reel	presupposes	visual and kinesthetic maps;
backwards	presupposes	visual and kinesthetic maps;
tripping	presupposes	visual and kinesthetic maps;
screaming	presupposes	an auditory map;
writhing	presupposes	kinesthetic and visual maps;
pain	presupposes	a kinesthetic map;
bitter	presupposes	gustatory and olfactory maps.

In addition to serving as a way of creating maps of the five representational systems, language also permits us to use it to create a model or a map of itself. For example, the previous sentence is a representation in a language system of one of the characteristics of that same representational system (language) — just like this one is. Language representational systems are reflexive, Meta representational systems. That is, we may create a language model of language itself as well as using it to create maps of the other five representational systems.

At this point, you may have noticed that it is easier for you to create an experience which is more vivid in one of these representational systems than in others. For instance, you may be able to close your eyes and see very clearly your closest friend but find it difficult to fully experience the smell of a rose. Or you may have found it easy to experience hearing a taxi horn, but found it very difficult to picture in your mind your closest friend. To some degree, each of us has, potentially, the ability to create maps in each of the five representational systems. However, we tend to use one or more of these representational systems as a map more often than the others. We also tend to have more distinctions available in this same representational system to code our experience, which is to say that we more highly value one or more of these representational systems.[2] For instance, those of you who have a highly valued visual representational system will have been able to close your eyes and vividly "see" a red square which became green and then blue. Also, you probably were able to make a very rich, clear picture of your closest friend. It is likely that you assume that other people who read this book will have this same experience. This is not true in all cases. The representational systems that are highly valued and highly developed in each of us will differ, either slightly or dramatically. Many people can make only vague pictures and some, no pictures at all. Some people must try for an extended period of time before they are capable of making a vivid image, and some can create a vivid image almost instantly. This wide variation in the capability to create a visual representation is also true of all the other representational systems.

Thus, each person's map or model of the world will differ both from the world and from the maps and models created by other people. Furthermore, each person will have a most highly valued representational system which will differ from the most highly valued representational system of some other person. From this fact — namely, that person *X* has a most highly valued representational system that differs from that of person *Y* — we can predict that each will have a dramatically different experience when faced with the "same" real world experience.

For example, when a musician listens to a piece of music, he has a more complex experience — he will be able to detect, represent and enjoy patterns of sound which will not be experienced by a person whose most highly developed system is visual (either consciously or behaviorally). A painter will be able to make distinctions in his experience of a sunset which are not available to a person whose most highly developed representational system is kinesthetic. A connoisseur of fine wines will detect subtle differences in the bouquet and flavor of distinct wines which cannot be detected by people whose most highly developed representational systems are not taste and smell used together.

IDENTIFYING THE MOST HIGHLY VALUED REPRESENTATIONAL SYSTEM

In order to identify which of the representational systems is the client's most highly valued one, the therapist needs only to pay attention to the predicates which the client uses to describe his experience. In describing his experience, the client makes choices (usually unconsciously) about which words best represent his experience. Among these words are a special set called *predicates*. Predicates are words used to describe the portions of a person's experience which correspond to the processes and relationships in that experience. Predicates appear as verbs, adjectives and adverbs in the sentences which the client uses to describe his experience. For example, in the following sentence, examples of each of these categories of predicates occur:

She saw the purple pajamas clearly.

The predicates in this sentence are:

        verb: *saw*
        adjective: *purple*
        adverb: *clearly*

EXERCISES

We will now present three exercises which will allow each of you to:

A. Sharpen your ability to identify predicates;
B. Determine the representational system or systems implied by each; and,
C. Become conscious of the predicates used by several specific persons.

EXERCISE A
Predicates

Identify the predicates in each of the sentences below.

He felt badly about the way she held the crawling child.

    verbs — *felt, held*
    adjective — *crawling*
    adverb — *badly*

The dazzling woman watched the silver car streak past the glittering display.

    verbs — *watched, streak*
    adjectives — *dazzling, silver, glittering*

He called out loudly as he heard the squeal of the tires of the car in the quiet streets.

    verbs — *called, heard*
    adjective — *quiet*
    adverb — *loudly*

The man touched the damp floor of the musty building.

    verb — *touched*
    adjectives — *damp, musty*

EXERCISE B
Representational Systems by Predicates

After you have identified the predicates in the above sentences, return to them and determine which representational system or systems each of them implies. Notice that some of them are ambiguous with respect to representational systems — for example, the predicate *light* may imply either a kinesthetic representational system or a visual one, depending upon its use. Or, the predicate *tighten* in a sentence such as:

She tightened her body.

may imply a visual or a kinesthetic representation, as I can verify the experience described in the sentence either by touch or by watching the muscle contractions of the person's body. One way to assist yourself when you are uncertain which representational system is involved is to ask yourself what you would have to do to verify the description given by the predicate and its sentence.

We would like to mention at this time that, in our training seminars, the common reaction which we receive to identifying highly valued representational systems by identifying predicates is one of disbelief. We would like you to realize that very little of natural language communication is really metaphorical. Most people, in describing their experiences, even in casual conversation, are quite literal. Comments such as "I see what you're saying" are most often communicated by people who organize their world primarily with pictures. These are people whose most highly valued representational system is visual. And they are literally "making pictures" out of what they hear. Our students first go through a stage of not believing this; secondly, they begin to listen to people in this new way and become amazed at what they can learn about themselves and those around them; thirdly, they learn the value of this knowledge.

We hope you will begin to listen to yourself and the people around you. Specifically, we ask you to do the following exercise to develop these new skills.

EXERCISE C
Identifying Predicates of a Specific Person

Choose one person each day and allow yourself to become conscious of this person's predicates; specifically, identify the representational system to which the predicates you hear belong. After allowing yourself to hear and to identify the person's representational system, ask him directly how he is organizing his experience at this point in time.

If the person's representational system is visual, ask the question:

> *Do you make pictures in your head?*
> *Do you have visual images in your head as you are talking and listening to me?*
> *Can you see what I am saying?*

If the person's representational system is kinesthetic, ask the questions:

> *Do you feel what you are saying?*
> *Are you in touch with what I am saying?*

If the person's representational system is auditory, ask the questions:

> *Do you hear voices in your head?*
> *Do you hear what I am saying inside your head?*

Try these exercises. We assure you that you can learn a great deal about yourself and the human beings around you. We urge you to ask any questions which will help you to understand the nature of how people organize their experiences in these different modes.

OUTPUT CHANNELS

Humans not only represent their experiences by different representational systems, they also base their communication on their representational systems. Communication occurs in a number of forms such as natural language, body posture, body movement, or in voice qualities, etc. We call them *output channels*. We will return to a discussion of these communication forms later in this book.

META — SO WHAT

SPEAKING THE CLIENT'S LANGUAGE

So far, we have described to you the various ways in which people organize their experiences by creating most highly valued representational systems such as visual, kinesthetic, auditory and natural language representational systems. This information about the way your clients organize their worlds, once understood, can be valuable to you in a number cf ways. First, a therapist's ability to understand more about how his clients experience and represent the world will enable him to better create experiences which they may use to change their lives. For example, in Chapter 6 of *Magic I*, we described a number of ways to assist the therapist in knowing when a particular technique is appropriate. For example, when the client has catastrophic fears of some future event for which he has no reference structure, a guided fantasy or spontaneous dream sequence could provide this reference structure. You might note at this point that fantasies will be more effective with visuals than with auditory people.

Next, consider how you, as a therapist, would decide to assist a client in an enactment — a replay of a past experience. If the client primarily organizes his experience visually (with pictures), then one way of helping to insure that he will have a way of representing the experience that the enactment creates is to have him choose other people to play the people in his past experience so that the client may actually see the enactment. If the client organizes his experience primarily kinesthetically (with body sensations), then having him actively play the people involved in his past experience will better assist him in setting the feeling (of all of the people) of the enactment.

As we pointed out in *Magic I*, one way in which people impoverish their world — limit themselves, take choices away from themselves — is by deleting a portion of their experience. When a person leaves out an entire representational system, his model and his experience are reduced. By identifying the client's representational system(s), the therapist knows what parts of the world, including the therapist, are available to the client. For example, if the client has some limitation in his model which is causing him pain, and the coping pattern which is blocking him from changing requires that he be able to represent his experience visually, then the therapist knows which kind of an experience to design to assist the client in changing. Assisting a client in recovering an old, or developing a new way of organizing his experience, whether being in touch, being clear sighted, or hearing acutely, is a powerful and moving experience for the client as well as for the therapist.

TRUST

A second, and probably the most important, result of comprehending your client's representational system is trust. Most psychotherapies place a high value on the client's trusting the therapist, but this is very rarely taught or explicitly understood. Your client will trust you when he believes that first, you understand him and, second, that you can help him to get more out of life. The important question, then, is, by what process does the client create this belief? This is closely connected to asking by what representational system clients organize their experiences. Suppose that we have a client who has a kinesthetic representational system. First, we listen to his description of his experience, then we check out our understanding of what he says (his model of the world) and phrase our questions — in fact, structure all of our communication with him — with kinesthetic predicates. Since this particular client organizes his experience kinesthetically, if we communicate with predicates that are kinesthetic, it will be easier for him both to understand our communication and to know (in this case, *feel*) that we understand him. This process of shifting predicates to allow our clients to understand our communication with greater ease is the basis and the beginning of trust. A client such as the one described above would *feel* that the therapist understood him, and would *feel* that, since the therapist was capable of understanding him, he was capable of helping him.

EXERCISE
Matching Predicates

Choose one person each day and determine by listening carefully to the predicates which he uses what is his most highly valued representational system. Then, using the translation table given below, adjust your own language responses to match his by using the response appropriate for his representational system. Use the table as follows: in the leftmost column is the meaning which you actually wish to communicate to this person; listed in the adjacent columns are the equivalents in the three representational systems.

Meaning	Kinesthetic	Visual	Auditory
I (don't) understand you.	What you are saying feels (doesn't feel) right to me.	I see (don't see) what you are saying.	I hear (don't hear) you clearly.
I want to communicate something to you.	I want you to be in touch with something.	I want to show you something (a picture of something).	I want you to listen carefully to what I say to you.
Describe more of your present experience to me.	Put me in touch with what you are feeling at this point in time.	Show me a clear picture of what you see at this point in time.	Tell me in more detail what you are saying at this point in time.
I like my experience of you and me at this point in time.	This feels really good to me. I feel really good about what we are doing.	This looks really bright and clear to me.	This sounds really good to me.
Do you understand what I am saying?	Does what I am putting you in touch with feel right to you?	Do you see what I am showing you?	Does what I am saying to you sound right to you?

By consciously selecting your predicates to match those of the person with whom you want to communicate, you will succeed in accomplishing clearer and more direct communications.

Once you can hear and understand the idea of representational systems, you then can make this piece of knowledge the basis of your knowing how to structure the experiences which you have with your clients. In this way, you can help them to begin to cope in new ways, which will make their lives better, and to fulfill their hopes and dreams to make their lives a more positive growth experience.

META-TACTICS

I. MATCHING OR NOT MATCHING PREDICATES

When you speak and when you ask questions of your clients, there is more going on than just an exchange of words. We devoted the whole first volume of *The Structure of Magic* to teaching how to ask questions based on the form of your clients' Surface Structure communications. The representational system which is presupposed by your clients' predicates is what we would call a *Meta-form*. If you want your client to understand and trust you, you have the choice of matching predicates. When you are seeking information from your client, phrasing questions with the appropriate presupposed representational system will enable the client to respond with greater ease and clarity. For example, when we are asking for information from a visual, we can phrase questions in the following ways:

How do you **see** *the situation?*
What do you **see** *stopping you?*

Or, when using the Meta-model with a kinesthetic, we will ask:

How do you **feel** *about this situation?*
What do you **feel** *stops you?*

Switching your predicates in this way will enable your clients to provide you with more information. We have, in past years (during in-service training seminars), noticed therapists who asked questions of their clients with no knowledge of representational systems used. Typically, they use only predicates of *their own* most highly valued representational systems. This is an example:

Client (visual): My husband just doesn't see me as a valuable person.

Therapist (kinesthetic): How do you feel about that?

Client (visual): What?

Therapist (kinesthetic): How do you feel about your husband's not feeling that you're a person?

Client (visual): That's a hard question. I just don't know.

This session went around and around until the therapist came out and said to the authors,

I feel *frustrated; this woman is just giving me a* **hard** *time.*
She's resisting everything I do.

We have heard and seen many long, valuable hours wasted by
therapists in this form of miscommunication with their clients.
The therapist in the above transcript was really trying to help, and
the client was truly trying to cooperate, but with neither of them
having a sensitivity to representational systems. Communication
between people under these conditions is usually haphazard and
tedious. The result is often name-calling, when a person attempts
to communicate with someone who uses different predicates.

Typically, kinesthetics complain that auditory and visual
people are insensitive. Visuals complain that auditories don't pay
attention to them because they don't make eye contact during the
conversation. Auditory people complain that kinesthetics don't
listen, etc. The outcome is usually that one group comes to
consider the other deliberately bad or mischievous or pathological.
However, we return to the basic premise of *Magic I:*

In coming to understand how people continue to cause
themselves pain and dissatisfaction, it is important to
realize that they are not bad, crazy or sick. They are, in
fact, making the best choice that they are aware of; that is,
the best choice available in their model of the world. In
other words, human beings' behavior, no matter how
bizarre it may seem, will make sense when it is viewed in
the context of the choices generated by their models.

If a person's model is visually based, his inability to answer a
question which presupposes a kinesthetic representation is not a
form of resistence but, rather, an indicator of the limits of his
model. His inability to answer such questions then becomes an
asset to the therapist, indicating the kind of experience which will
help the client expand his model. Since this particular client's
model of the world was primarily visual, the lack of kinesthetic
and auditory representational systems could be the source of her
dissatisfaction with her husband. In fact, this turned out to be
true. The authors took the therapist back into a session and
proceeded to elicit the following information.

The woman knew her husband didn't *see* her as valuable.
Therapist: How do you know he doesn't see you as
valuable?
Client: I *dress up* for him and he doesn't *notice.* (The
client is assuming her husband also has a visual model

of the world, as she does.)

Therapist: How do you know he doesn't notice?

Client: He just paws me and doesn't even look. (He responds kinesthetically and doesn't stand back far enough to see.)

The therapist could now begin the process of teaching this woman that her map is not the territory in two ways: first, she can learn that her husband experiences the world differently from her and that her mind reading (see *Magic I,* Chapter 4) is not her husband's reality. He may, in fact, have noticed her and is responding to her according to his model of the world (i.e., kinesthetically). Second, the therapist may begin the process of developing in this woman a kinesthetic representational system which will expand her map of the world in many new ways.

One of the ways to accomplish this is by deliberately matching predicates instead of haphazardly using unmatched predicates. The therapist may ask the woman in the above transcript:

> How do you **feel** *as you* **see** *your husband not noticing you?*

The therapist recognizes as he asks this question that the client may not be able to answer it. If the client fails to repond, the therapist may then begin instructing her in developing a kinesthetic representational system.

Therapist: Close your eyes and now make a picture of your husband. Can you see him? (Client nods.) Good; now describe what you see.

Client: He is just sitting in a chair, ignoring me.

Therapist: As you look at this image, become aware of any body sensations in your stomach or tightness in your back or arms. What do you feel as you look?

Client: I'm not sure.

Therapist: Well, describe it as best you can.

Client: I guess my back is a little stiff, and . . .

Time spent in this way will allow your clients, like this woman, to develop representational systems for their maps. This, of necessity, will increase their models of the world in a way that allows them new choices. For too long, different approaches to psychotherapy have pushed *right* answers. Some therapies have criticized auditory representation as being analytical and have said that they need to be more in touch. Our experience has been that we need all our potential will offer — kinesthetic, visual and auditory. The techniques and forms of all the psychotherapies offer a vast resource to accomplish this goal. Many therapies offer techniques which put people more in touch. Many offer techniques which enable people to clearly see what goes on in their lives, and still others help people to hear.

This kind of methodical use of all of the approaches to therapy can only result in your being effective with a larger number of your clients in a more consistent way.

II. SWITCHING REPRESENTATIONAL SYSTEMS

As we repeatedly pointed out in *Magic I,* when people come to us in therapy with pain, feeling that they are stuck, that they don't have enough choices, we find that their world is rich and varied enough for them to get what they want, but that the way which they use to represent the world to themselves is *not* rich and varied enough for them to obtain it. In other words, the way that each of us represents our experience will either cause us pain or allow us an exciting, living and growing process in our lives. More specifically, if we choose (consciously or not) to represent certain kinds of experience in one or another of our representational systems, we will succeed either in causing ourselves pain or in giving ourselves new choices. The following are examples of this process. Notice that, in each case, the Meta-Tactic of switching representational systems allows the client to overcome the pain or the block to further growth and change.

George, a young man in his late 20's, volunteered to work in a group setting (a Therapist Training Group). He was asked to come to the center of the group, sit down, and state on what he wanted to work. He began a rather rambling account of the events of his day, and then, wincing in pain, interrupted his story to complain about a severe headache which had been troubling him for some hours. He stated that he was unable to concentrate on his story because of the pain from his headache. The therapist decided to deal directly with the physical (kinesthetic) representation by using Meta-Tactic II. Having listened carefully to George's choice of predicates while he was making his complaints, the therapist recognized, from statements such as the following, that George's most highly valued representational system was visual.

I don't see *what my headache has to . . .*
I try to watch out *for things that . . .*
I'm not clear *right now. If I could only* focus *on what . . .*

The therapist then placed an empty chair in front of the chair in which George was sitting, and said:

Therapist: George, look at the chair in front of you; see that, at this point in time, it is empty. Now, allow your eyes to close, maintaining a clear, focused image in your mind's eye of the empty chair in front of you. Now paint me a picture of your headache with words as vivid and colorful as possible. I want you to see the exact way that your muscles are interlaced, straining and causing you this pain. Do you have a clear picture?

George: Yes, I see it clearly. (George goes on to describe the headache in visual terms, with the therapist asking questions [with visual predicates] to assist him in picturing it.)

Therapist: Now, George, breathe deeply and rhythmically. (Here the therapist moves to George and verbally and kinesthetically [by touch] assists him in developing a deep and rhythmic breathing pattern.) Now, George, I want you to see clearly as you breathe out, with each breath, breathing out, to breathe out all of the pain in your headache. I want you to see the headache slowly dissolving and flowing from your head, through your nasal passages, now through your nose and flowing out of your nostrils with each deep breath out, breathing out, breathing this cloud of flowing, swirling pain into the empty chair in front of you, see it there, make a focused image of it in the chair as you breathe it out deeply. Signal me by nodding when you focus the cloud of pain in the chair in front of you in your mind's eye.

George signaled, by nodding, that he had accomplished this. The therapist then assisted him in creating a face and body from this swirling cloud of pain in the chair in front of him. The face and body belonged to someone with whom George had some unexpressed, unfinished business. After George had expressed himself to this person, the therapist leaned forward and asked him how he felt at that particular point in time. George smiled, and, with a surprised look on his face, replied:

Why, I feel *fine, completely focused — my headache is completely gone!!*

This particular process, of working with a young man who had a severe headache, required only a few minutes. The process is simply an example of the effective use of Meta-Tactic II. What we have noticed is that, if people represent certain kinds of experiences in their kinesthetic representational systems, they succeed in causing themselves pain. As in this case, if the therapist is able to determine the client's most highly valued representational system other than kinesthetic, then the therapist will be able to assist the client in re-mapping (or re-coding or re-representing) the experience which is causing him pain from the kinesthetic system into another highly valued representational system. In other words, the therapist assists the client in switching an experience from the representational system which is causing pain into one which will not result in pain, and will occur in a form with which the client can better cope. The generalization, then, from this case and others very like it is that, when a client is experiencing pain (equivalent to a message that he has represented some experience kinesthetically in a way which is causing him pain), the therapist may choose to deal with that pain directly by:

    (a) Identifying the person's most highly valued representational system (other than kinesthetic);

    (b) Creating an experience whereby the client maps *from* the kinesthetic representation *into* his most highly valued system.

Thus,

$$\text{Kinesthetic representation} \longrightarrow \left\{ \begin{array}{l} \text{Visual representation} \\ \text{Auditory representation} \\ \text{Digital representation} \end{array} \right\}$$

Notice that the Meta-model itself is understood to be the mapping function which carries an experience from any representational system into a digital (words, phrases and sentences) representation.

Thus,

$$\left\{ \begin{array}{l} \text{Visual representation} \\ \text{Auditory representation} \\ \text{Kinesthetic representation} \end{array} \right\} \xrightarrow{\text{Meta-Model}} \text{Digital representation}$$

Susan, a woman in her late 30's, asked to work one evening in the context of a Therapist Training Group which we were conducting. She was asked to come to the center of the group and state on what she wished to work. She said that she had been troubled by vivid images in her mind. She said that she had tried to get rid of these images but that they continued to haunt her, making her unable to do many of the things which she wanted to do. By listening carefully to the woman's choice of predicates, the therapist was able to identify the kinesthetic as the client's most highly valued representational system. Susan was then asked to describe the images which she had been having in as much detail, as vividly, as possible. Once she had completed her description, the therapist had her go through the entire sequence again, and this time he had Susan act out each of the parts of her visual images kinesthetically — that is, she became the parts of her visual fantasy and experienced them directly in her body. The entire process took about 20 minutes, and, at the end of the enactment, Susan stated that the visual images which had been persecuting her were gone and that she felt a tremendous increase in her strength.

This second episode again demonstrates the power of using Meta-Tactic II. In this case, a woman whose primary representational system was kinesthetic was experiencing difficulty in coping with a series of visual images. By assisting her in mapping her experiences in her visual representational system into her most highly valued representational system (kinesthetic), the experiences were brought into a form with which she was able to cope, and she could then use them as a source of strength for herself. The generalization here is that, when a client is having difficulty coping with some experience in a representational system other than her most highly valued one, then one excellent choice on the part of the therapist is to assist her in re-mapping that experience into her most highly valued system. A person's most highly valued system is the one in which he has the maximum number of distinctions, and usually is the one in which he will be able to cope most effectively.

Thus,

Representational System X ⟶ Representational System Y

where Y is the client's most highly valued representational system.

III. ADDING REPRESENTATIONAL SYSTEMS

The third of the Meta-Tactics available to therapists in their use of representational systems is that of simply adding to the client's reference structure another representational system. By adding an entirely new representational system, the client's model of the world is dramatically extended and many new choices become available to him. Consider the change in the experience of a person who has been organizing his experience wholly in terms of body sensations (kinesthetically) when he is suddenly able also to represent his experience visually. This change literally allows him a new perspective on life, a new way of having choices about his life. Meta-Tactic III differs from Meta-Tactic II in that, rather than map an experience from one representational system into another representational system, in this case we have the person retain his experience in the present representational system and simply *add* another entire representation of this same experience.

Mary Lou, a woman in her middle 40's, was working in a Therapist Training Group. As Mary Lou was expressing her difficulties, the therapist noticed that, each time she expressed some comment critical of her own behavior, Mary Lou's voice quality (tonality) changed. She spoke, literally, with a different voice. The therapist then asked Mary Lou to repeat a number of the critical remarks and, as she did so, to be aware of her voice. When she finished repeating the critical remarks, the therapist leaned forward and asked her whose voice she had used. She replied at once that it was her father's voice. At this point, the therapist asked her to close her eyes and to hear that same voice inside her head. She was able to do this easily. Next, the therapist instructed her that, as she listened to her father's voice, she would see her father's mouth moving, his lips forming the words. As she accomplished this, she was then instructed to see the remainder of her father's face.

The therapist continued to work with Mary Lou, using her father's voice to lead her in constructing a full visual representation which matched the voice she continued to hear inside her head. Once the visual and auditory representations were coordinated, the therapist used the material as a basis for an enactment in which Mary Lou played both herself and her father. Thus, in this final phase, all three representational systems were brought into play — auditory, visual and kinesthetic. The enactment technique, based upon initially using an auditory representation and then adding the other representational systems (visual and kinesthetic) to it — that is, Meta-Tactic III — enabled Mary Lou to confront and overcome some severe blocks to her further growth.

This experience with Mary Lou shows the use of Meta-Tactic III. The therapist notices a sudden shift in a client's behavior. Making use of the representational system in which this sudden shift occurs as a basis from which to build a more complete reference structure (See *Magic I*, Chapter 6), the therapist finds a point of overlap between the representational system in which the shift took place and the representational system which the therapist chooses to add. In this case, since the initial representational system was auditory (specifically, the voice of another person), the therapist had the client form a visual image of the mouth which was creating that voice. Once a portion of the new representational system is tied to the initial representational system, the therapist can work with the client to fully develop the new representational system. The consequence of this Meta-Tactic is to expand dramatically the client's representation of the experience which is causing him difficulty. This expanded representation allows the client an expanded model of the world and, from this, more choices in coping in his life. The generalization, then, for Meta-Tactic III can be represented as:

(a) Selecting an experience which is registered in representational system X with which the client is having difficulty coping;
(b) Finding a point of overlap between representational system X and representational system Y pertaining to that experience;
(c) Fully developing the experience initially represented in X in the new representational system Y;
(d) Repeating step (b).

Symbolically:

$$\text{Representational System X} \longrightarrow \begin{cases} \text{Representational System X} \\ \text{Representational System Y} \\ \text{Representational System Z} \end{cases}$$

SUMMARY OF PART I

The statement by Korzybski that "the map is not the territory" is true in two major ways. First, we, as humans, create models of our world which we use as a guide for our behavior. Second, we have a number of different maps available to represent our experiences — kinesthetic, visual, auditory, natural language, etc.[3] These maps of our experience do not necessarily represent *only* information from the direct input channels of the senses to the associated representational systems. For example, I can describe a picture in natural language and another person can hear my description and make pictures of this description. We, as humans, usually have a most highly valued representational system, and very often we will neglect to use the additional representational systems available to us.

A most highly valued representational system can be identified by listening to the natural language predicates used by a person in describing his experience. Trust results when the therapist joins his clients in their representational systems and then switches his predicates to theirs; this is, in essence, speaking the clients' language. (Trust has more components than just switching predicates — these will be discussed later.)

Once you, as a therapist, understand how your client organizes his experience, which representational system is used and which is the client's most highly valued one, then you can proceed in therapy in a way which will be strategically more beneficial in expanding your client's model of the world in a way which will allow him more choices, greater freedom in living, and a richer life overall.

FOOTNOTES FOR PART 1

1. We talk here about major input channels. Our experience leads us to believe that we all are constantly receiving information through at least the five commonly identified input channels — vision, hearing, touch, smell, and taste. We distinguish the three channels of vision, hearing and touch as the major channels, as these are the ones which provide information which, typically, enters our consciousness. One strong piece of evidence that we are also receiving information through the other two channels comes from the activation of survival responses — for example, the smell of smoke enters consciousness almost immediately and the person smelling it will begin to search for its source, disregarding his previous activity. Furthermore, in our work in both therapy and hypnosis, we have noticed that the experience of

certain tastes and smells allows the person experiencing them to return to associated childhood memories immediately. The neural set of pathways carrying olfactory information is the only set of pathways of the five senses which does not pass through the thalmus en route to the cerebral cortex. We are also convinced that people receive information through processes other than those associated with the five commonly accepted senses.

2.   By most highly valued representational system we mean the representational system the person typically uses to bring information into consciousness — that is, the one he typically uses to represent the world and his experience to himself. As we shall present in detail in Part II of this volume, a person may have more than one most highly valued representational system, alternating them. This is common in people who are incongruent in their communication — the polarity game. Again, no special one of the representational systems available is better than the others, although some may be more efficient for certain tasks. In our work, the general, overall strategy we use is to assist people in having available to them choices about how they organize their experiences.

3.   Others could exist. Also, we use smell and taste for recovering old, especially childhood, memories and for certain survival responses; e.g., the *smell* of fire.

PART II
Incongruity

THE TASK OF THE PEOPLE-HELPERS

Two human beings sit facing one another. One is called a therapist and the other, a client. This second person, the client, is unhappy, dissatisfied with his present life; feels stuck, blocked; experiences pain in his life. The therapist is faced with the task of assisting the client to change in a way which will allow him to grow, allow him more choices, more satisfaction, and less pain in his life. What, exactly, is the task that the therapist, this people-helper, will accomplish when he assists the client in changing?

Our understanding of the task of a people-helper is:

> All therapies are confronted with the problem of responding adequately to such people. Responding adequately in this context means to us assisting in changing the clients' experience in some way which enriches it. Rarely do therapies accomplish this by changing the world. Their approach, then, is typically to change the clients' experience of the world. People do not operate directly on the world, but operate necessarily on the world through their perception or model of the world. Therapies, then, characteristically operate to change the client's model of the world and, consequently, the client's behavior and experience. . . . The overall strategy that the therapist has adopted is that specified explicitly by the Meta-Model — to challenge and expand the impoverished portions of the client's model. Characteristically this takes the form of either recovering (enactment) or creating (guided fantasy, therapeutic double bind, . . .) a reference structure which contradicts the limiting generalizations in the client's model.
>
> (*Magic I*, Chapter 6)

In other words, the therapist will work to create an experience with the active, creative participation of the client. This experience will be directed at the way in which the client has organized his perception or model of the world which is blocking him from changing. This experience will lie outside the limits of the client's model. The process of creating and living this experience will provide the client with a new model and a new set of choices for his life.

MULTIPLE MESSAGES

There are a number of ways which a therapist may choose in going about creating this experience. In this section of the book, we will present a series of choices which a therapist has available when dealing with one particular category of behavior in his clients. Here we focus on a phenomenon called *incongruity*.

In Part I of this volume, *Representational Systems*, we detailed the different maps we as human beings use to organize our experience. Since each of us has the means of organizing our experience in different representational systems, the question arises as to whether these representational systems not only have different *types of information*, but also have different *models of the world* for the same person. In the past few decades, psychotherapy has begun to pay attention not only to the communication of the client with words, but also his communication by body language. The notion of multiple messages has begun to be the basis of much work in this area.

Let's return to these two humans (the therapist and the client) and watch and listen for a moment.

The client and the therapist have been working together for about twenty minutes. The client has been discussing his relationship with his wife. The therapist leans forward and asks the client what his feelings are toward his wife at this point in time. The man immediately stiffens his body, cuts his breathing dramatically, thrusts his left hand forward with his index finger extended, drops his right hand into his lap with its palm turned upward, and says, in a harsh, shrill tone of voice at a rapid rate of speech:

I do everything I can to help her; I love her so very much.

Consider the messages that the therapist is receiving from the client at this point:

a. Body stiff;
b. Breathing shallow and irregular;
c. Left hand thrust forward with extended index finger;
d. Right hand palm open and turned up in lap;
e. Harsh, shrill voice;
f. Rapid rate of speech;
g. The words: *I do everything I can to help her; I love her so very much.*

This description is one of a person who is communicating

incongruently — that is, the messages carried by his various output channels (body posture, movements, voice tempo, voice tonality, and words) do not fit together to convey a single message. For example, the client's words stating his love for his wife do not match the tonality of his voice as he says these words. Again, the client's left hand with the extended index finger does not match his right hand held palm open and turned up in his lap. The message carried by the client's words is different from the message carried by the client's tonality. The message carried by the client's left hand is different from the message carried by his right hand.

The therapist is faced at this point with a client who is presenting him with a set of messages which do not match (an incongruent communication). He is confronted with the problem of responding adequately to these multiple messages. We trust that each of you reading this description (of a client communicating incongruently) can identify situations in which you, yourself, have been confronted with a client who is presenting you with multiple, incongruent messages. Let us consider for a moment the choices which are available to the therapist (or anyone responding to a person who is communicating incompatible messages).

First, the therapist may fail to detect (consciously) the incongruities — the non-matching messages being presented by the client. Our observations of this situation are that, when a therapist fails to detect incongruities which the client is presenting, the therapist himself, initially, feels confused and uncertain. The therapist's feelings of uncertainty usually persist and he becomes more and more uncomfortable. Typically, therapists report feeling as though they were missing something. What we have observed in our Therapist Training Seminars is that, in a remarkably short period of time, the therapist, himself, will begin to respond incongruently. More specifically, the therapist will tend to match with the client the kinds of messages which he is receiving, output channel for output channel.

Using the above description as an example, the therapist who fails to detect the incongruencies described will soon find himself talking to the client about his feelings of love and devotion to his wife in a voice which is harsh, and, at the same time, he will begin to register incongruities in his body posture which match the client's incongruities. For example, his hand gestures will not match each other. Thus, this first *choice* is no choice at all; rather, it is a failure on the part of the therapist to detect the multiple messages which the client is presenting.

Secondly, the therapist may detect the client's conflicting messages and may choose to regard one or the other of these as the valid, or true, message which *really* conveys the client's *true* feelings about his wife. Our experience with therapists who make this choice is that their acceptance of an output channel message as the *true* one is based upon the context of the message. For example, there is a general cultural rule which states that each of us may respond (consciously) only to the *words* which a person uses to describe his experience, not to the other output channels (tonality, posture, etc.). Responding to the messages carried by output channels other than verbal is, in general, impolite, or "dirty pool," as one of our acquaintances characterized it. Thus, we are taught, culturally, that the valid message in the set of simultaneous, non-matching messages a person communicating incongruently presents to us is the verbal message.[1] Many of the psychotherapies have selected (implicitly, at least) the message carried by body posture and gesture as the *real* or *true* message for the client — the opposite of the choice given to us culturally. A therapist trained in one of these schools will select one of the messages carried by the client's body posture or gestures as the one to which he should respond. Once a therapist has decided which of these conflicting messages is the valid one, he has the choice either of deciding what the message carried by that particular output channel *really means* (by *really means* we are referring to the words the posture or gesture would have if it were translated into language), or of calling the client's attention to that message in some way, and then requesting that the client inform the therapist of the meaning of the message carried by that output channel.

The first choice on the part of the therapist we refer to as an *hallucination.* By hallucination we are not implying a value judgment that this is a bad or negative move on the part of the therapist, but simply that, when a therapist decides without checking with the client what the meaning of a non-verbal message is in words, he is assuming that the meaning of that posture or gesture in words is the same as it is in *his own* model of the world. The meaning that the posture or gesture has in the therapist's model of the world may or may not match the meaning that that posture or gesture has in the client's model of the world. As we stated in *Magic I:*

> ... therapist may, from long experience, have an intuition about what the missing piece is (in this case, what the meaning of the posture or gesture is). He may choose to

interpret or guess. . . . We have no quarrel with this choice. There is, however, the danger that any form of interpretation or guessing may be inaccurate. We include in our Meta-model a safeguard for the client. The client tries the interpretation or guess by the therapist by generating a sentence which includes that material and checks his intuitions to see whether it fits, makes sense, is an accurate representation of his model of the world.

The second possibility — that of selecting one of the non-verbal messages as the *valid* one and asking the client to express it in words — is a choice which we have already discussed in the first part of this book. Specifically, this move is a request by the therapist for the client to switch representational systems. Here, the therapist is instructing the client to switch from a message carried by body posture or gesture to a message carried by the language representational system.

The choice described above made by our therapist — that is, selecting the message carried by the body output system as the valid representation of the client's *true* feelings — has a strong basis in theories of communication and therapy.

THEORY OF LOGICAL TYPES

In our understanding, the most explicit and sophisticated model of human communication and therapy is that described in the work of Gregory Bateson and his colleagues. Bateson, using his wide-ranging background and penetrating mind, developed, for example, the Double Bind Theory of Schizophrenia. In formulating this theory, Bateson borrowed a model first presented by Bertrand Russell to cope with certain paradoxes arising in meta-mathematics; this model is called the Theory of Logical Types.

CONTENT AND RELATIONSHIP

Bateson and his colleagues categorize each human communication into two parts or "levels." These are called the *content* and the *relationship* messages. More specifically, the verbal (digital) portion of the communication (or what the person says *in words*) is considered the content message of the communication, while the non-verbal (analogical) portion of the communication is considered the relationship message. The following diagram will help you to understand the relationship between Bateson's terminology and that which we use.

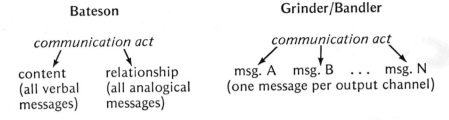

Using the example previously given, we have the following classification:

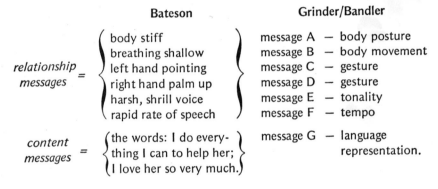

In addition to classifying the client's communication into the two categories of content and relationship, Bateson offers the following method to determine which category of a message is the valid one:

> When a boy says to a girl, "I love you," he is using words to convey that which is more convincingly conveyed by his tone of voice and his movements, and the girl, if she has any sense, will pay more attention to those accompanying signs than to the words.
>
> *(Steps to an Ecology of Mind,* p. 412)

Or, as Bateson comments:

> What is known to occur at the animal level is the simultaneous presentation of contradictory signals — postures which mention both aggression and flight, and the like. These ambiguities are, however, quite different from the

phenomenon familiar among humans where the friendliness of a man's words may be contradicted by the tension or aggressiveness of his voice or posture. The man is engaging in a sort of deceit, an altogether more complex achievement.

(Steps to an Ecology of Mind, pp. 424-25)

In both of these statements, Bateson implies that the relationship part of the communication — the portion carried by the non-verbal part — is the valid portion of the communication when there is a difference or an incongruity. In fact, in the latter quote, he uses the word *deceit* to describe the use of words by a human to convey a message which differs from the message carried by the non-verbal portion of the communication. His use of this word presupposes that the non-verbal or analogical message is the one which faithfully reflects the *true* nature of the person's feelings and intentions. This choice on the part of Bateson and therapists in general becomes more understandable when we examine the model which they are using to organize their experience in therapy — the Theory of Logical Types.

In his adaption of Russell's Theory of Logical Types to communication and therapy, Bateson chose to assign the *relationship* portion of the communication — the message carried by the non-verbal part — to a level higher than the *content* portion of the communication. In other words, the analogical, non-verbal message is considered meta to — of a higher logical type than — the verbal message. A message, call it A, will be considered meta to some other message (B) if message A is a comment on B, or if, equivalently, A contains B as one of its parts (less than the entirety of A), or, equivalently, if A includes B in its scope (A is about B). An example will help. A client says:

I feel angry about my job. (= message B)

The therapist responds by asking:

How do you feel about feeling angry?

The client responds:

I feel frightened about feeling angry about my job.
(= message A)

The client's statement, message A, is about the client's statement, message B; therefore, message A is meta to message B. Message A is a meta-message with respect to message B.

Russell developed the Theory of Logical Types to avoid paradoxes. His theory is that, once statements (or whatever category of things was being considered) were sorted out by logical type, they were to be kept separate under pain of paradox — that is, to mix statements (or any objects) of different logical types was to invite paradox — a form of pathology to which mathematicians are particularly vulnerable. Consequently, when Bateson adapted Russell's theory, he accepted this generalization that objects (in this particular case, messages) of different logical types or different logical levels are to be kept separate.

Specifically, Bateson assigned the relationship portion or analogical part of the communication act to a meta position with respect to the content or verbal portion of the communication — the body posture/movement/tonality/tempo message was a comment on the verbal message. Thus, the analogical and the verbal portions of every communication are of different logical types. We can represent this classification visually as:

Bateson's use of Russell Theory

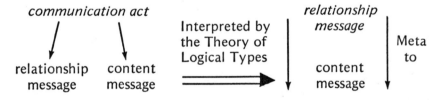

PARAMESSAGES

We have found the following way of organizing our experience in therapy and communication more useful in assisting clients in changing: The client presents a set of messages, as many as one per output channel. These messages we call *paramessages*. No one of these simultaneously presented messages is meta to any one of the others presented. More generally, then, no one of a set of simultaneously presented messages can be of a different logical level from any other. Visually, we represent this classification by the following diagram:

Grinder/Bandler Schema

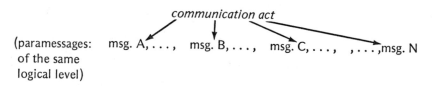

communication act

(paramessages: msg. A, . . . ,   msg. B, . . . ,   msg. C, . . . ,   , . . . ,msg. N
of the same
logical level)

There are three major differences between Bateson's model and this way of organizing our experience in therapy and communication. First, we distinguish one (possible) message per output channel, whereas Bateson's schema is binary, dividing the messages into a relationship (analogical) and a content (verbal) portion. Our method allows us to check for incongruity among the multiple messages. The binary split, however, allowing only a single check for congruency (analogical versus verbal), doesn't allow for the case (which we encounter very often) wherein, the various ways which a human can use to express messages analogically themselves do not match, i.e., are incongruent. The case which we mentioned previously contained several examples of this phenomenon:

the left hand with its index   *versus*   the right hand palm open
finger extended   and turned up on the lap
or
the right hand palm open   *versus*   the harsh, shrill voice
and turned up in the lap

Thus, we have generalized Bateson's binary schema into an n-ary schema (n is the number of output channels available to carry messages).[2] This generalization allows us to check for incongruency among all of the different messages which the client presents to us. Thus, Bateson's schema can be seen as a special case of ours in which all of the analogical paramessages match.

The second major way in which we have found it useful to organize our experience in communication and therapy which differs from Bateson's schema is that, in any set of simultaneously presented messages, we accept each message as an equally valid representation of that person's experience. In our model, no one of these paramessages can be said to be more valid — or truer, or more representative of the client — than any other. No one of a set of paramessages can be said to be meta to any other member of its set.[3] Rather, our understanding of a set of paramessages is that each of these messages represents a portion of the client's model(s) of the world. When the client is communicating congruently, each of the paramessages matches, fits with, is congruent with each of the others. This tells us that all of the models which the client is using to guide his behavior at that point in time are consistent (or, equivalently, that the client is using a single model of the world). When the client presents us with a set of conflicting paramessages, when the client is communicating incongruently, we know that the models of the world which he is using to guide his behavior are inconsistent. We accept each of the conflicting paramessages as a valid representation of the model which the client has for his behavior — these conflicting paramessages are indicators of the resources which the client has in coping with the world. When incongruity is seen in this way, the problem of deciding which of the conflicting messages presented to us simultaneously is the real, true or valid message disappears and such incongruencies, themselves, become the basis for growth and change.

In addition to the increased therapeutic possibilities which this way of organizing our experience gives us, we have been unable to find any specific case in our experience in which one of a set of paramessages is meta with respect to any other. For example, in the case we described previously, in what sense is the left hand with the index finger extended a comment on, or a message about, the words which the client says? Our experience has been that the words used by the client are as usefully considered a comment on, or a message about, the message conveyed by the left hand with the index finger extended as vice versa. Thus, we arrive at a classification of paramessages — messages of the same logical level. Using this organization, we avoid one difficulty which arises in Bateson's schema, that of deciding which of a set of paramessages is meta to the others. One case in which the futility of attempting to make this decision is particularly clear is that in which a client is both incongruent at a particular point in time and incongruent over a period of time and, thus, the messages are reversed. Specifically, one of the members of our Therapist Training Seminars was working on some patterns she had developed in her original family system. As with many, if not all, of us who have had two adults acting as our parents, her parents differed about how their child should be treated. And, as is the case with many, if not all, of us, the child was faced with the formidable task of integrating the conflicting messages she had received as a child from her parents. As one of the seminar participants began to work with her on these patterns, he noticed the following: When Ellen was addressing her father (fantasized), she either stood erect, feet spread apart, left hand on her hip, right arm and hand extended with finger pointing, voice whining and with a typical statement such as,

> *I try as hard as I can to please you, Daddy; just tell me what you want me to do.*

or, she stood slumped, with her feet together, both arms and hands extended, palms turned upward, voice loud, harsh and low, and with typical statements such as,

> *Why don't you ever do what I want you to do?*

Extracting these patterns into a table form, we see:

Ellen at Time 1		Ellen at Time 2	
erect posture	msg. A1	slumped posture	msg. A2
feet spread	msg. B1	feet together	msg. B2
left hand on hip	msg. C1	both arms and hands extended,	msg. C2
right arm and hand extended, with index finger pointing	msg. D1	palms turned upward	
whining voice	msg. E1	voice loud and harsh	msg. E2
words: *I try as hard as I can to please you, daddy . . .*	msg. F1	words: *Why don't you ever do what I want you to do?*	msg. F2

In the Bateson schema, the therapist is faced with several difficulties. First, he must decide at Time 1 which of the messages which Ellen is presenting is the valid one. Since, in this binary schema, the relationship message is meta to the content message (words), it constitutes the real or valid message about Ellen's relationship to her father. There is a difficulty here as the messages carried by the analogical systems, themselves, do not agree; specifically:

msg. A, B, C, and D   *versus*   msg. E

(body postures and   (voice quality)
gestures)

Suppose, however, that, since the majority of the non-verbal messages agree, we pass over this difficulty and decide that the message carried by body posture and gestures is the true or valid representation of Ellen's relationship to her father. Now, the second difficulty arises. At Time 2, Ellen's communication has changed radically. Specifically, if you compare the messages at Time 1 and Time 2 pairwise (body posture at Time 1 with body posture at Time 2), they are absolutely reversed. Thus, when Ellen is communicating at Time 2, the therapist, using the same principles, is forced to arrive at an understanding of Ellen's relationship to her father which is in conflict with what he had decided, based upon her communication at Time 1.

Using the model which we proposed previously, no difficulties arise for this case of Ellen and her relationship to her father. At both Time 1 and Time 2, Ellen is incongruent — at both times, the set of paramessages do not fit but, rather, are arranged as follows:

	Ellen at Time 1		**Ellen at Time 2**
	messages A1, B1, C1, and D1 are congruent (first set)		messages A2, B2, and C2 are congruent (first set)
and		**and**	
	messages E1 and F1 are congruent (second set)		messages E2 and F2
and		**and**	
	the first set of paramessages is not congruent with the second set		the first set of paramessages is not congruent with the second set

What makes Ellen's communication particularly interesting is that the first set of messages at Time 1 is congruent with the second set of messages at Time 2, while the second set of messages at Time 1 is congruent with the first set of messages at Time 2. In other words, Ellen's analogical (discounting voice quality temporarily) messages at Time 1 fit her verbal messages at Time 2 and vice versa. Since in the paramessage system all messages are treated as equally valid, the difficulty never arises — Ellen's case (a reasonably familiar one in our experience) is easily understood. Ellen has two models of her relationship to her father — she experiences pain and lack of choice, and her behavior is not consistent with respect to her father, as these two models are, at this point in time, inconsistent. Both are, however, equally valid expressions of her *true* feelings toward her father — both constitute resources for Ellen, parts of her which she can integrate. We will return to Ellen's case later in this section to demonstrate the strategy of integration.

We propose to continue to use the meta distinction in our model. However, for some message (A) to be labeled meta to some other message (B), two conditions must be met:

A message (A) will be labeled meta to a message (B) if and *only if:*

    (a) Both A and B are messages in the same representational system or same output channel;

and

    (b) A is a message about B (equivalently, A has B in its scope — the Bateson/Russell condition).

Notice now that, since, as we stated previously, each output channel may carry one and only one message at a time, messages which are presented simultaneously will never be meta one to the other. Condition (a) insures this, as it states that the metamessage relationship can only occur between messages expressed in the same representational or output system.[4] Therefore, it naturally follows that paramessages (the set of messages presented simultaneously by a person) will never be meta with respect to one another.

Retaining the meta distinction is useful for us in our work. Consider, for example, the following case: A client is describing his feelings about his work experience. As he says, in a low, whining tone of voice,

I really am beginning to enjoy my job.

he clenches both of his fists, first raising and then bringing his left fist down on the arm of the chair. The therapist chooses to metacomment on these pieces of analogical (body gesture and voice) communication. The therapist leans forward and says,

> *I heard you say that you are really beginning to enjoy your job, and, as you said this, I was aware of two other things: your voice didn't sound like you are enjoying your job, and you balled your hands up into fists and hit the arm of your chair with your left fist.*

In terms of the model which we have developed, the therapist has succeeded in metacommenting. Specifically, he metacommented on three messages presented by the client:

Client's Messages:
> The words: *I really am beginning to enjoy my job.*
> The client's voice tone as translated by the therapist into the words: *Your voice didn't sound like you are enjoying your job.*
> The client's body movement as translated by the therapist into the words: *You balled your hands up into fists and hit the arm of your chair with your left fist.*

Therapist's Metacomment or Metamessage:
> The words: *I heard you say that you are really beginning to enjoy your job, and, as you said this, I was aware of two other things: your voice didn't sound like you are enjoying your job, and you balled your hands up into fists and hit the arm of your chair with your left fist.*

The therapist's metamessage meets both of the conditions we presented above — it is in the same representational system as the client's messages, and it is a message about the client's messages. Notice that, in order to successfully present a metamessage to the client, the therapist had to translate the client's messages (presented in output systems [voice tone and body movement] other than the one which the therapist intended to use to present the metamessage [language]) into that output system — the therapist translated the client's non-verbal behavior which he wished to comment on into words and then commented on that behavior in words. The therapist has employed the representational systems Meta-Tactic II (Switching Representational Systems) as an essential part of his metamessage.

The third way in which our model of incongruity differs from the Bateson model is that, since in the paramessage set no message is meta with respect to any other, there are no restrictions on the integration of the parts of the person represented by these para-messages when they are incongruent. In the binary model in which all relationship (analogical) messages are meta with respect to the content (digital) messages, any attempt to integrate the parts of the person represented by these conflicting messages is automatically a violation of the Theory of Logical Types. Thus, in the context of this model, such an attempt at integration invites paradox. We will return to this point later in the section on integration. In table form, then, we can show the three major ways in which our model for incongruity differs from that developed by Bateson and his colleagues:

Grinder/Bandler	Bateson/Russell
n-ary distinctions available for congruity checks (para-messages).	Binary distinctions available for congruity checks (meta-message—message).
Accepts all output channel messages as valid representations of the client.	Distinguishes the relationship level (analogical) as meta to the content level (verbal) and, therefore, is the valid message.
Accepts no restrictions on integration of parts of the client represented by the differing paramessages.	Accepts a restriction on integration of parts of the person — any attempt to integrate parts represented by relationship and content levels is a violation of the Theory of Logical Types.

We move on now to a presentation of the strategy for using a client's incongruities as a basis for growth and change.

A GENERAL STRATEGY
FOR RESPONDING TO INCONGRUITY

When a client communicates incongruently, presenting a set of paramessages which do not match, the therapist is faced with an existential decision. The therapist's actions in responding to the incongruency of the client will have a profound effect upon the client's subsequent experience.

The therapist's task in working with a client's incongruencies is to assist the client in changing by integrating the parts of the client which are in conflict, the incongruencies which are draining his energies and blocking him from getting what he wants. Typically, when a client has parts which are in conflict, no part is successful, but each sabotages the others' efforts to achieve what they want. Within a client who has conflicting parts, there are (at least) two incompatible models or maps of the world. As these models both serve as a guide for the client's behavior and are incompatible, his behavior is, itself, inconsistent. Integration is a process by which the client creates a new model of the world which includes both of the formerly incompatible models in such a way that they are coordinated and function smoothly together, both working to assist the client in getting what he wants from life.

The general strategy for integrating conflicting parts in a client is stated in *Magic I* (Chapter 6, pp. 28-29):

> Different portions of a person's reference structure can be expressed by different representational systems ... the portion of the reference structure which one representational system is expressing does not fit with the portion of the reference structure which the other representational system is expressing — we refer to this situation as an inconsistent double message, incongruity or incongruent communication. ... One of the most impoverishing situations which we have encountered in therapy is that in which a person maintains contradictory portions of his reference structure. Typically, these contradictory portions have the form of two contradictory generalizations which apply to the same area of behavior. Most frequently, the person whose reference structure includes these inconsistent generalizations has the experience of being immobilized, being profoundly confused, or oscillating between two inconsistent forms of behavior.
>
> ... the overall strategy that the therapist has adopted is that specified explicitly by the Meta-model — to challenge and expand the impoverished portions of the client's model. Characteristically, this takes the form of either recovering (enactment) or creating (guided fantasy, thera-

peutic double bind) a reference structure which contra-
dicts and therefore challenges the limiting generalizations
in the client's model. In this case, the incongruent communication itself is an indicator of the two portions of a
person's inconsistent reference structure — two generalizations which can serve as contradictory reference structures
for each other. The therapist's strategy here is to bring the
two contradictory generalizations into contact. This can be
most directly accomplished by bringing these generalizations into the same representational system.

More specifically, the strategy for working with incongruities
involves three phases:

1. *Identifying* the client's incongruencies;
2. *Sorting* the client's incongruencies;
3. *Integrating* the client's incongruencies.

These three phases are, of course, a fiction, as are all models. It
sometimes happens that the phases do not occur in their full form,
or, frequently, they will not be sharply distinguishable, but will
flow into one another. They have proven to be, as is demanded of
any model, a useful way both of organizing our own experiences
in therapy and in teaching others to do the same.

In short, the therapist has the task of assisting the client in
learning to use his conflicting parts or incongruencies as resources
— of assisting the client to become congruent.

To assist the reader in following the description of the three
phases of work in incongruity, we provide here a mini-glossary.

Mini-Glossary

Congruency/Incongruency — The term *congruency* is used to
describe a situation in which the person communicating has
aligned all of his output channels so that each of them is
representing, carrying or conveying the same or a compatible
message. When all of a person's output channels (body posture
and movements, voice tonality and tempo, words) are representing the same or compatible messages, the person is said to
be congruent. Other people's experience of a congruent human
being is usually described in terms of that person's having
personal presence, knowing what he is talking about, being
charismatic, dynamic, and a host of other superlatives. Two

outstanding examples which come to our minds of people who have developed this ability to be congruent are the well-known family therapist Virginia Satir and Rudolf Nureyev, one of the world's best known dancers.

The term *incongruent*, then, applies to a situation in which the person communicating is presenting a set of messages carried by his output channels which do not match, are not compatible — this person is said to be incongruent. Other people's experience of an incongruent person is confusion, saying that he doesn't know what he really wants, is inconsistent, untrustworthy, indecisive.

The terms *congruent* and *incongruent* may be applied to messages presented by a person's output channels as well as to the persons themselves. Thus, if messages carried by two output systems are incompatible, do not fit, do not match, they are incongruent; if they fit, they are congruent.

Finally, the terms *congruent/incongruent* may be applied to representations in different representational systems using the same criteria as stated above.

Metamessage/Paramessage — The term *metamessage* is applied to a message (A) with respect to some other message (B) if two conditions hold:

Message A is meta with respect to message B if and only if:
    (a) Both A and B are messages in the same representational system or in the same output channel

and
    (b) A is a message about B (equivalently, A has B in its scope).

For example, if message B is the sentence *I feel angry*, then message A is considered meta with respect to B, when A is the sentence *I feel scared about feeling angry*.

The term paramessage is applied to two or more messages expressed simultaneously in different representational systems or (more usually) in different output channels. Paramessages may be either congruent or incongruent with respect to one another. For example, if a woman says the sentence *I am sad* with a voice tone which is loud and threatening, the messages represented by the words *I am sad* and the voice tonality are paramessages, in this case incongruent paramessages. Paramessages are always messages of the same logical level, expressed in different representational systems or output channels.

Consistent/Contradictory — The term *consistent* is applied to two or more messages of the same logical type (expressed in the same representational system or output channel) which are compatible — they can both be true at the same time. For example, the statements

> *I am hungry.*

and

> *I want to eat.*

are consistent messages.

The term *contradictory* is applied to two or more messages of the same logical type (expressed in the same representational system or output channel) which are incompatible — they cannot both be true at the same time. For example, any sentence and its negation; the sentences

> *I'm hungry.*

and

> *I'm not hungry.*

are such a pair.

Satir Category/Stance — Virginia Satir has identified four communication categories or stances which people adopt under stress. Each of these Satir categories are characterized by a particular body posture, set of gestures, accompanying body sensations, and syntax.

(1) *Placater*
Words — agree — ("Whatever you want is okay. I am just here to make you happy.")
Body — placates — ("I am helpless.")
Insides — ("I feel like a nothing; without him I am dead. I am worthless.")

The *placater* always talks in an ingratiating way, trying to please, apologizing, never disagreeing, no matter what. He's a "yes man." He talks as though he could do nothing for himself; he must always get someone to approve of him. You will find later that if you play this role for even five minutes, you will begin to feel nauseous and want to vomit.

A big help in doing a good placating job is to think of yourself as really worth nothing. You are lucky just to be allowed to eat. You owe everybody gratitude, and you really are responsible for everything that goes wrong. You know you could have stopped the rain if you used your brains, but you don't have any. Naturally you will agree with any criticism made about you. You are, of course, grateful for the fact that anyone even talks to you, no matter what they say or how they say it. You would not think of asking anything for yourself. After all, who are you to ask? Besides, if you can just be good enough it will come by itself.

Be the most syrupy, martyrish, bootlicking person you can be. Think of yourself as being physically down on one knee, wobbling a bit, putting out one hand in a begging fashion, and be sure to have your head up so your neck will hurt and your eyes will become strained so in no time at all you will begin to get a headache.

When you talk in this position your voice will be whiny and squeaky because you keep your body in such a lowered position that you don't have enough air to keep a rich, full voice. You will be saying "yes" to everything, no matter what you feel or think. The placating stance is the body position that matches the placating response.

(2) *Blamer*

Words — disagree — ("You never do anything right. What is the matter with you?")

Body — blames — ("I am the boss around here.")

Insides — ("I am lonely and unsuccessful.")

The *blamer* is a fault-finder, a dictator, a boss. He acts superior, and he seems to be saying, "If it weren't for you, everything would be all right." The internal feeling is one of tightness in the muscles and in the organs. Meanwhile the blood pressure is increasing. The voice is hard, tight, and often shrill and loud.

Good blaming requires you to be as loud and tyrannical as you can. Cut everything and everyone down.

As a blamer it would be helpful to think of yourself pointing your finger accusingly and to start your sentences with "You never do this or you always do that or why do you always or why do you never . . ." and so on. Don't bother about an answer. That is unimportant. The blamer is much more interested in throwing his weight around than really finding out about anything.

Whether you know it or not, when you are blaming you are breathing in little tight spurts, or holding your breath altogether, because your throat muscles are so tight. Have you ever seen a really first-rate blamer whose eyes were bulging, neck muscles and nostrils standing out, who

was getting red and whose voice sounded like someone shoveling coal? Think of yourself standing with one hand on your hip and the other arm extended with your index finger pointed straight out. Your face is screwed up, your lips curled, your nostrils flared as you yell, call names, and criticize everything under the sun.

(3) *Computer*

Words — ultra-reasonable — ("If one were to observe carefully, one might notice the workworn hands of someone present here.")

Body — computes — ("I'm calm, cool, and collected.")

Insides — ("I feel vulnerable.")

The *computer* is very correct, very reasonable with no semblance of any feeling showing. He is calm, cool, and collected. He could be compared to an actual computer or a dictionary. The body feels dry, often cool, and disassociated. The voice is a dry monotone, and the words are likely to be abstract.

When you are a computer, use the longest words possible, even if you aren't sure of their meanings. You will at least sound intelligent. After one paragraph no one will be listening anyway. To get yourself really in the mood for this role, imagine that your spine is a long, heavy

steel rod reaching from your buttocks to the nape of your neck, and you have a ten-inch-wide iron collar around your neck. Keep everything about yourself as motionless as possible, including your mouth. You will have to try hard to keep your hands from moving, but do it.

When you are computing, your voice will naturally go dead because you have no feeling from the cranium down. Your mind is bent on being careful not to move, and you are kept busy choosing the right words. After all, you should never make a mistake. The sad part of this role is that it seems to represent an ideal goal for many people. "Say the right words; show no feeling; don't react."

(4) *Distracter*
Words — irrelevant — (the words make no sense)
Body — angular and off somewhere else
Insides — ("Nobody cares. There is no place for me.")

Whatever the *distracter* does or says is irrelevant to what anyone else is saying or doing. He never makes a response to the point. His internal feeling is one of dizziness. The voice can be singsong, often out of tune with the words, and can go up and down without reason because it is focused nowhere.

When you play the distracting role, it will help you to think of yourself as a kind of lopsided top, constantly spinning, but never knowing where you are going, and not realizing it when you get there. You are too busy moving your mouth, your body, your arms, your legs. Make sure you are never on the point with your words. Ignore everyone's questions; maybe come back with one of your own on a different subject. Take a piece of imaginary lint off someone's garment, untie shoelaces, and so on.

Think of your body as going off in different directions at once. Put your knees together in an exaggerated, knock-kneed fashion. This will bring your buttocks out and make it easy for you to hunch your shoulders and have your arms and hands going in opposite directions.

At first this role seems like a relief, but after a few minutes of play, the terrible loneliness and purposelessness arise. If you can keep yourself moving fast enough, you won't notice it so much.

As practice for yourself, take the four physical stances I have described, hold them for just sixty seconds and see what happens to you. Since many people are unaccustomed to feeling their body reactions, you may find at first that you are so busy thinking you aren't feeling. Keep at it, and you will begin to have the internal feelings you've experienced so many times before. Then the moment you are on your own two feet and are freely relaxed and able to move, you find your internal feeling changes.

It is my hunch that these ways of communicating are learned early in childhood. As the child tries to make his way through the complicated and often threatening world in which he finds himself, he uses one or another of these means of communicating. After enough use he can no longer distinguish his response from his feeling of worth or his personality.

Use of any of these four responses forges another ring in an individual's feeling of low self-worth or low pot. Attitudes prevalent in our society also reinforce these ways of communicating — many of which are learned at our mother's knee.

"Don't impose; it's selfish to ask for things for yourself," helps to reinforce placating.

"Don't let anyone put you down; don't be a coward," helps to reinforce blaming.

"Don't be so serious. Live it up! Who cares?" helps to reinforce distracting.

(*Peoplemaking,* pp. 63-72;
Science and Behavior Books)

Finally, we would add to Satir's excellent description of each of these communication stances the syntactic correlates which we have found to accompany them:

Satir Category 1 — Placater
Use of qualifiers: *if, only, just, even,* etc. Use of subjunctive mood of verbs: *could, would,* etc. Mind reading violations.

Satir Category 2 — Blamer
Use of universal quantifiers: *all, every, any, each time,* etc. Use of negative questions: *Why don't you? How come you can't?* etc. Cause-Effect violations.

Satir Category 3 — Computer (super-reasonable)
Deletion of experiencer noun arguments — the subject of active verbs as in *I see — as can be seen* or the object of verbs wherein the object noun argument is the experiencer as in *disturbs me — X is disturbing.* Use of nouns without referential indices: *it, one, people,* etc. Use of nominalizations: *frustration, stress, tension,* etc.

Satir Category 4 — Distracter
This category, in our experience, is a rapid alternation of the first three; thus, the syntax which identifies it is a rapid alternation of the syntactic patterns of each of the three listed above. Also, the client displaying this category rarely uses pronouns in his responses which refer to parts of the therapist's sentences and questions.

PHASE 1
IDENTIFYING THE CLIENT'S INCONGRUITIES

The first step in the overall strategy for working with incongruencies is for the therapist to be able to recognize incongruencies in the client's communication. Each time a client expresses himself, he uses each of his output channels to represent to the therapist a message or set of messages. As we discussed previously, each output channel conveys one message — the set of all messages presented simultaneously is called *paramessages*. Each of these paramessages is a valid representation of the client at that point in time. If each of the output channels carries the same message, then the client and the set of paramessages are congruent. If, however, one or more of the output channels conveys a paramessage which does not fit with the paramessage carried by another of the output channels, the client is incongruent. In order for therapists to detect incongruency in clients, therapists must have the ability to use their sensory input channels without hallucinating. Specifically, the therapist can come to recognize the paramessages being presented by the various body postures and gestures/movements of the client's body both visually and kinesthetically. The therapist can use both of his eyes and his hands and other parts of his body to watch and to touch the client's body. The therapist uses his auditory input channel to listen to the sounds which the client produces. The therapist checks both within each of his input channels and across input channels to determine whether or not the paramessages which he is receiving match. For example, within the auditory input channel, the therapist checks the words which the client utters against the voice tone, against the tempo or rate of speech which the client uses to convey his experience. If the therapist determines that the three messages carried to him in the auditory input channel match, he then checks these paramessages against the paramessages he is receiving through his visual and kinesthetic input channels to determine whether these are all congruent, one with the other.

We are not suggesting that the distinctions which we are describing here exhaust the possible distinctions which we are capable of making as human beings — for example, in the auditory input channel that language, tonality and tempo are the only, or even the most important, distinctions which a therapist can make in therapy to detect incongruencies. What we are identifying here are some of the distinctions which we have found useful for ourselves both in our work and in teaching others to become skilled therapists. Furthermore, we want to point out that experienced therapists rarely consciously check within and then among their different input channels to determine whether the client is communicating congruently. Rather, as we have come to realize in our experiences in Therapist Training Seminars, people training to become therapists initially rely primarily on a few distinctions in one or more of their input systems. During this initial period, they are very conscious of checking these distinctions. However, in a relatively short period of time, this systematic checking of a few distinctions in one or more input channels drops out of their consciousness, but their behavior remains systematic — that is, they continue to consistently detect incongruities in the client's communication when conflicting paramessages are presented along these distinctions. In other words, while they no longer consciously check for conflicting messages from the client in these dimensions, they continue to see, hear and feel incongruities. Typically, after they have mastered these first distinctions and these drop out of consciousness, they begin to hear, see and feel new distinctions which allow them to make even more subtle judgments about the congruency of the client's communication.

We want once more to emphasize that the therapist during this phase of incongruency work with the client is not attempting to interpret or understand the meanings of the various paramessages which the client produces as he communicates, but is making a simple congruent/not congruent comparison among the paramessages which he is receiving.[5]

There is to our knowledge no way for therapists to detect incongruencies in the client's communication except for therapists to develop their abilities to see, hear and feel without hallucinating. Once a therapist has trained herself to have her input channels free to accept the paramessages presented by the client and to compare them for congruency, she is well on her way to becoming a dynamic and effective therapist. We have in the course of our Therapist Training Seminars developed a number of special techniques which people training themselves to become therapists have found useful. These are simply special cases of the general principles which we have already presented — there is no substitute for clearing and developing your input channels. We present three of these special cases.

Case I — "but"

Sometimes the therapist hears the client utter a sentence and he suspects that he heard some incongruity but is not certain. One of the most common of these cases is when the client utters sentences such as:

> *I really want to change the way that I act in public.*
> *I actually don't want to go to the party.*
> *I truly want to go to the show with him tonight.*

In English, when a person says a sentence which is a simple statement his voice drops at the end of the sentence. Say the following two sentences aloud and listen to the difference in the way your voice shifts at the end of the sentence.

I will leave home precisely at midnight.
and
Do you want to leave home precisely at midnight?

In saying the second sentence (the question) aloud and listening to yourself, you will have noticed that your voice rose at the end, while, when you said the first sentence, your voice dropped at the end. Now, say the first set of sentences again, this time allowing your voice to rise slightly at the end — not as dramatically as you did with the question but do not allow your voice to drop as is customary with simple statements. Listen to this first set of sentences as you say them. If you have said them with the correct intonation pattern (slight rise at the end), you will have an almost-an-incongruity experience. People whose most highly valued representational system is auditory will, in fact, hear an additional word inside their heads after the last word of each of the first set of sentences — specifically, they will hear the word *but*. This is the basis of the almost-an-incongruity experience. What has happened is that the slight rise in intonation at the end of this special class of sentences called Implied Causatives (see *Magic I*, Chapter 4, for a detailed discussion) signals the listener that the sentence is not complete — a portion of it is missing. Whenever you are acting as a therapist and have this particular experience, we suggest that you simply lean forward, look carefully at the client and say the word *but* and wait for the client to finish the sentence with the portion which he had originally omitted. Thus,

> Client: I really want to change the way that I act in public.
> Therapist: . . . but . . .
> Client: . . . but I'm afraid that people won't pay attention to me.

This provides an excellent opportunity for you to train your input channels to notice differences in the client's communication. Typically, the client's body posture, gestures, tonality, tempo and syntax will be radically different during the period when he is saying the portion of the sentence before you, the therapist, say the word *but* and during the period when he is saying the portion of the sentence after you say the word *but*. In other words, the client will express two different parts or models of the world —

one associated with the first portion of the sentence and another associated with the last portion of the sentence.

Case II — The Meta-Question

Another very common situation which we have found useful for assisting people in learning to identify shifts or differences in the client's communication is what we have termed the meta-question. The following is an example:

> *Client:* I feel so angry about my job.
> *Therapist:* Yes, and how do you feel about feeling angry?
> *Client:* Well, I feel scared about feeling angry.

This question is extensively used by Virginia Satir in her dynamic therapy — she describes this question as an excellent way to tap the client's self-esteem (the client's feelings about his feelings) — a part of the client closely connected with his ability to cope (see *Magic I*, Chapter 6, for more discussion). Again this exchange typically involves the client's shifting the paramessages in each of his output channels radically from his first statement about his feelings to his response to the therapist's meta-question about his feelings about his feelings — the next higher logical level. We will return to this example during the section on integration to demonstrate effective ways for a therapist to cope with different parts of a client which exist (at this point in the process) as different logical types — one meta to the other.

Case III — An Anatomical Basis for Incongruity

It has been known for some time that the vast majority of right-handed human beings have their language function located in their left cerebral hemisphere. This assymetry is perhaps the most widely accepted of the differences which have been claimed to exist between the two hemispheres of the brains of human beings. One of the most fascinating reports concerning the possibility of independent action by each hemisphere individually comes from studies of people whose major connection between the cerebral hemispheres has been severed surgically. Some of the medical personnel involved are convinced that the result of such operations leaves the person operated on with two independent, only tenuously associated, consciousnesses (see Gazzaniga, Eccles in the bibliography). Gazzaniga comments (pp. 106-07):

> ... other cases, where the will and intent of one hemi-
> sphere (and usually the left) could prevail over the entire
> motor system, antagonistic behavior between the two
> halves of the body was kept at a minimum. Case I, how-
> ever, would sometimes find himself pulling his pants down
> with one hand and pulling them up with the other. Once,
> he grabbed his wife with his left hand and shook her
> violently, while with the right trying to come to his wife's
> aid in bringing the left belligerent hand under control.

We have become aware that bi-lateral incongruities exist in many of the communications of our clients when the words which the client is saying are congruent with the paramessages being expressed by the right side of the client's body while the left side (in a client who is right-handed) is carrying a set of paramessages which are incongruent with the verbal paramessage and the communications carried on the opposite side. For example, a fairly common incongruity is what we have come to call *the choker* — typically, the client's words and the right side of his body are carrying messages which are congruent while the client's left hand is fastened tightly on his throat, blocking much of the available passage for the flow of air. Paying close attention to the paramessages being carried by the words and the right side of the client's body and comparing them to the paramessages being conveyed by the left side will provide you with a continuing opportunity to sharpen your ability to detect incongruities.[6]

In this, the final portion of Phase I — Identifying the Client's Incongruity — we present you with a series of exercises. These exercises are designed to assist you in developing your skill in detecting incongruencies — an important skill in your growth as a people-helper.

EXERCISES
DEVELOPING YOUR ABILITY
TO DETECT INCONGRUENCIES

VISUALLY

During your waking hours you are constantly being bombarded with visual information; much of this is visual information about other human beings like yourself. This exercise is designed to assist you in sharpening your skills in identifying incongruent paramessages visually. Decide at the beginning of each day before leaving your home to set aside a 30-minute period some time during the day for you to exercise your ability to identify incongruent visual communications. Decide on a specific time and place — the place should allow you to observe people conversing with one another without your becoming involved in the conversation. Observing from a distance of between 5 and 20 feet will be satisfactory — a public place such as a cafe, a restaurant, an airport, or a park will do.

Step 1 — When you arrive at the place you have decided upon, find yourself a comfortable position, take out a pad and pencil, and take a deep breath. Select one person to observe, giving this person your full attention for the first 10 minutes. Ignore all sounds, especially any sounds which the person you're observing might be making. On your pad of paper, you will have copied the list of visual checkpoints listed at the end of this exercise. Begin by consciously and systematically considering each of the first three items on the checklist; take your time and check each in turn, comparing the paramessages being conveyed by each of these items on your checklist to see whether they are congruent with one another. If you find that you have no difficulty determining whether the first three items on your checklist are conveying congruent paramessages, increase the number of checklist items until you are using all the items on the checklist. After the first 10 minutes, select another person to observe, following the above sequence. Repeat a third time. Compare your experience in observing these three people.

Step 2 — When you have done the exercise described in Step 1 above each day for a week or when you find that you can perform that exercise with ease, try the following: Again decide on a time and place for your exercise — the same requirements as in Step 1. Again select a person to observe. This time, however, use the checkpoint list for each side of the body — that is, in the case of checking the hands of the person whom you are observing, check the paramessages conveyed by position and movements of the right hand against the paramessages presented by the position and movements of the left hand. Next check the set of paramessages carried by all of the checkpoints on one side of the person's body against the set of paramessages carried by the other side. Spend the first 15 minutes doing this. In the last 15 minutes, observe another person — this time do *not* use the checklist; rather, focus your eyes on a spot 3-4 feet to one side or the other of the person (find some object to focus on at that distance). Notice that you are able to detect the client's movement move accurately when focusing your eyes in this way — pay particular attention to the smoothness (or lack of it) of the person's movement, whether the person completes his movements or cuts them short, whether one side of his body moves in a manner congruent with the way the other side of his body moves. Spend 5 minutes in this type of observation. For the remaining 10 minutes, simply observe the person without the use of the prepared checklist, note any portions of the person's body which are particularly expressive for your purposes of identifying incongruencies. You will find, for example, that certain portions of the body of the person you are observing move in unison as though rigidly connected together while other portions of his body move independently of one another.

Continue this exercise for a week or until you can do it with ease.

Checklist for Visual Paramessages
1. The person's hands;
2. The person's breathing;
3. The person's legs and feet;
4. The eye fixation patterns;
5. The head/neck/shoulder relationship;
6. The facial expression, especially the eyebrows, the mouth, and the cheek muscles.

AUDITORIALLY

As with your visual sense, during your waking hours you are constantly being bombarded with auditory information. This exercise is designed to assist you in refining your skills in identifying incongruent paramessages auditorially. As in the instructions given for the first exercise, decide at the beginning of each day for a week before leaving home to set aside a 30-minute period in which you will exercise your new skill. Decide on a specific time and place — again, this place should allow you to sit near enough (5—10 feet, depending on noise level) that you can hear distinctly the voice of the person to whom you will be listening. Places such as those suggested for the visual exercise will serve your purposes here.

When you arrive at the place which you have selected, find yourself a comfortable position, take out a pad and pencil, and take a deep breath. Choose one person to listen to — listen to this person with your full and complete attention. To assist you in accomplishing this, either unfocus your eyes, close them, or focus them on some non-moving, homogeneous portion of the place you're in — a blank wall, for example. Ignore all visual input; concentrate your attention on the person you have selected. On your pad of paper you will have copied the list of auditory distinctions to which you are to pay attention. Go through the first three items on your list, consciously and systematically considering each of these one by one. Then compare them pairwise to determine whether the paramessages which are being conveyed are congruent or not. If you find that you have no difficulty in making congruency judgments about these paramessages, increase the number of checklist items that you are using until you are using all of them. Use 10 minutes of your total 30 minutes in this way. Repeat the exercise with two more people. Compare the patterns of congruency and incongruency among the paramessages of the people whom you have observed.

Checklist for Auditory Paramessages
1. The tonality of the person's voice;
2. The tempo of the person's speech;
3. The words, phrases, and sentences used by the person;
4. The volume of the person's voice;
5. The intonation patterns of the person's speech.

VISUALLY AND AUDITORIALLY

Repeat the initial preparations as in the previous two exercises — decide on a place and time and allow yourself 30 minutes a day for a week for this exercise. This is designed to give you practice in comparing paramessages in different modalities for congruency. Place yourself so that you are able to both see and hear the person you have selected. Begin by checking for congruency among the first three items on your visual checklist, then check the first three items on your auditory checklist, and, finally, check the items across checklists. increase the number of paramessages from each list until you are using both lists. Observe and listen to three people for 10 minutes each. Compare the patterns of congruency and incongruency for each of these people. Once this task has become easy for you, begin to pay particular attention to the congruency/incongruency patterns as discussed in Case III — An

Anatomical Basis for Incongruency. Specifically, notice the congruency/incongruency patterns of handedness, verbal para-messages, and the paramessages which are displayed in those postures and movements of the side of the person's body which is controlled primarily by the dominant hemisphere.

PHASE 2
SORTING THE CLIENT'S INCONGRUITIES

When a client presents a therapist with a set of incongruent paramessages, he has, quite literally, presented the therapist with a set of choices of how to proceed to assist him in changing and growing. Each paramessage is a statement to the therapist that the client has a resource which the therapist may choose to use in the client's growth process. The therapist, by recognizing each of these paramessages as a valid representation of the client, is accepting and utilizing the client's resources in a way which avoids judgments about what is *best* for the client or about which of the conflicting paramessages is the *true* representation of the client.[5] It is at this point — when the therapist has identified the incongruities in the client's communication — that the therapist will begin to work actively to convert the client's incongruities into identifiable, fully expressed parts. Here one of the important choices which the therapist must make is how many and which of the client's parts he will assist the client in integrating. Our experience in this task ranges from working with two parts to up to twenty parts simultaneously.

POLARITIES

The most common sorting of a client's incongruities is a sorting into two parts — we distinguish this situation with a special name. When a client's incongruent paramessages are sorted into two parts for therapeutic work, we call these two parts *polarities*. Very dramatic therapeutic work and profound and lasting change can be achieved by a therapist and clients through polarities.

Simultaneous Incongruity

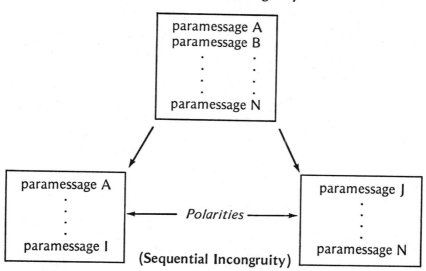

We recommend the sorting of incongruities into polarities as an excellent therapeutic technique and one which will allow the therapist to make sense out of the client's behavior. We make effective polarity work a prerequisite for therapists before instructing them in working with more than two of the client's identifiable parts at one time. In our description of Phases 2 and 3, we will focus on the two-parts situation — the polarity case; the remarks we make are also applicable to work in which more than two parts are being handled simultaneously. At the end of the sections on Phases 2 and 3, we will discuss more specifically working with more than two parts at a time.

INCONGRUITIES INTO POLARITIES

The therapist is now ready to help the client to sort his incongruities into polarities. He begins by selecting one of the paramessages with which the client has presented him. Suppose we use a description given earlier in this part as an example. The messages which we identified earlier (coming from a male client) were:

Body stiff (Paramessage A);
Breathing shallow and irregular (Paramessage B);

Left hand with extended index finger (Paramessage C);
Right hand palm open and turned up in lap (Paramessage D);
Harsh, shrill voice (Paramessage E);
Rapid rate of speech (Paramessage F);
The words: *I do everything I can to help her; I love her so very much* (Paramessage G).

What we have here is a set of paramessages which do not match — the client is being incongruent. The therapist does not, at this point, interpret the paramessages; he simply notes that they do not *all* fit. However, some of the paramessages fit with other paramessages. For example:

Group I	Group II
Left hand with extended index finger;	Right hand palm open, turned up in lap;
Harsh, shrill voice; Rapid rate of speech;	The words: *I do everything I can to help her; I love her so very much.*

The paramessages in Group I fit with one another as do the paramessages in Group II. The paramessages of one group do not, however, fit with those of the other group. (The paramessages not listed in either Group I or Group II fit with either group.) The client has, of course, had long experience in expressing his *mixed feelings* about his wife and will, in most cases, be quite unaware of the incongruities in his communication. The therapist now selects one of the groups of paramessages which fit together and begins the process of assisting the client in fully expressing one of his polarities. Suppose that the therapist chooses to work with the Group II paramessages first. He arranges two empty chairs, facing one another. He directs the client to sit in one of these chairs and tells him to repeat what he has just said. As the client repeats the words which he had just said, the therapist listens and watches carefully — his task now is to teach the client to be totally congruent in his communication, using the Group II paramessages as a guide. In other words, as the client repeats what he originally said, the therapist acts as a movie director or a play director, coaching the client, providing feedback, literally molding the client's body with his hands and words, instructing him in voice tonality and rate of speech until all of the client's output channels are representing the same or congruent paramessages. He then directs the client to move over into the opposite chair, leaving behind all the feelings and thoughts which he has just expressed. The therapist places the client's body in the posture and with the gestures which he identified as Group I paramessages. After placing him in this body posture, the therapist directs the client to say something which fits for him at that moment in time, and to say it with a rapid rate of speech and in a harsh, shrill voice. The therapist utilizes his skills in detecting incongruities to change the portions of the client's communication (the paramessages) which do not fit with the paramessages of Group I. In other words, the therapist now uses the paramessages of Group I as the guide and adjusts all of the client's other paramessages to be congruent with these. Here he is working to have the other polarity express itself fully and congruently. The therapist will usually have to have the client switch from chair to chair (that is, from polarity to polarity) a number of times before he will be able to express himself congruently in each position.

What have the therapist and the client accomplished when the client is able to express himself congruently in each polarity? One way of answering this question which we have found useful in our Therapist Training Seminars is to state that the client has changed from expressing himself *incongruently simultaneously* to expressing himself *incongruently sequentially*. The client began the session stuck and confused, incongruent in his communication, simultaneously expressing parts of himself which did not fit together. Now the client can express himself congruently at each *point* in time, although he is still incongruent over a *period* of time. The situation has changed from one of simultaneous incongruity to sequential incongruity, or *alternating polarities*. When this occurs, the second phase of the incongruity work is accomplished.

In the description of the therapist's actions in sorting incongruencies into polarities, we simply stated that he worked with the client to assist him in communicating congruently in each polarity, assisting him in expressing each of his polarities fully, one after the other. We will now present some explicit techniques for assisting the client in moving from simultaneous incongruities to alternating polarities. We will consider three specific problems in sorting incongruities into polarities which we have noted occurring over and over again:

(1) How to sort incongruities into polarities — what techniques are effective in shifting from a set of incongruent paramessages to polarities;

(2) How to assist the client in fully expressing each polarity;

(3) How to know, specifically, when the polarities are sorted for integration.

Spatial Sorting

In the example described above, we used a technique which was made famous by the late Fritz Perls — the "empty-chair" technique. The therapist in the example used two chairs as locations which the client could associate with each of his polarities. This empty-chair technique is only one of a potentially infinite number of ways of sorting incongruencies into polarities on the basis of *spatial sorting*. Each of you can use your own imagination to create a variation on the empty-chair technique. The underlying principle is to use a distinct spatial location to assist the client in sorting the paramessages into polarities — two different patterns on a rug, two sides of a doorway, etc. Each of these would serve equally well. The most useful part of the technique is that it helps both the therapist and the client to know where each paramessage is located. Notice that spatial sorting always actively involves the client kinesthetically — that is, the client must physically move from one spatial location to another. This actual kinesthetic change (especially when used with instructions from the therapist to leave behind all of the feelings and thoughts [of one polarity] expressed in that spatial location when moving to another) is congruent with the change that the client is learning to make, allowing first one polarity and then the other to express itself without incongruent paramessages between the polarities.

Fantasy Sorting

A second useful way to organize incongruities into polarities is *fantasy sorting*. This is particularly useful with clients whose most highly valued representational system is visual. Using the above example again, the therapist, having detected the groupings of the paramessages, decides to use Group II as a guide: He instructs the client to allow his eyes to close and to make a picture of himself down on one knee with his hands extended, palms turned up. Once the client has indicated that he has a stable, clear, focused image of himself, the therapist will begin to add other paramessages congruent with those of Group II already incorporated into the image, both in the same representational system (visual) — for example, a quivering lip[7] and in other representational systems as well. For example, the therapist may say:

As you watch your lips move, hear the words: "I do

everything I can for her; I love her so very much."

Now the therapist has the client report the entire image, checking it for incongruent paramessages. When the image is congruent, the therapist works with the client to create a second visual fantasy, this time a congruent image of the other polarity (based on the client's paramessages in Group I). The therapist will usually have to instruct the client to switch the images several times until each is congruent. With this fantasy sorting, the client has access to visual and auditory presentations of his polarities in a way that he does not have in spatial sorting.[8]

Psychodramatic Sorting

A third technique which we have found useful in sorting is one which we call *psychodramatic sorting*. Here the therapist has the client select two members of the group to play his polarities. With the assistance of the therapist, the client instructs first one and then the other person in playing his polarities. For example, the therapist has one of the group members adopt all of the para-messages in Group I while the other group member adopts all of the paramessages of Group II. The client and the therapist then work with the selected group members to make each of them a fully expressed and congruent polarity. This sorting technique gives the client an opportunity to experience his polarities visually and auditorially. During the course of instructing the group members to play the polarities properly (that is, in a way which matches the client's models), the therapist will direct the client to play first one and then the other of the polarities. This provides the opportunity for the client to experience his polarities kines-thetically as well as to insure that the group members are playing his polarities properly. The psychodramatic sorting technique serves as an excellent training device to assist therapists in training to detect, sort, and reproduce the paramessages presented by the client.

Representational System Sorting

A fourth and extremely powerful technique for assisting a client in sorting incongruities into polarities is that of *represen-tational system sorting*. One of the most frequent ways which people use in maintaining inconsistent models of the world — the basis for incongruities, and, therefore, polarities — is by repre-senting the conflicting portions of their model(s) in different representational systems. We can utilize this principle effectively in the sorting phase of incongruity work with clients. For example, the therapist may choose to have the client sit in one of the empty chairs and, using Group II paramessages as a starting point, require that the client report all of his feelings (body sensations — kinesthetic representational system) about his wife. Here the therapist is alert to the predicates which the client uses, instructing him in the use of kinesthetic predicates to report his feelings. Once the client has described his feelings, the therapist will move him and have him report his images and visual perceptions of his experience with his wife. Here the therapist assists the client in using visual predicates in reporting. One specific way to do this would be for the therapist to assist the client in re-enacting a recent unsatisfactory experience that he had with his wife. The client reports all of the body sensations which he experienced; he then reports all of the pictures — the visual information he has of the experience. We encourage the people in our Therapist Training Seminars to use this technique in conjunction with the following one — that of *Satir Category Sorting* — and have found it amazingly potent.

Satir Category Sorting

To use a Satir Category Sorting technique, the therapist simply sorts the paramessages available into the Satir Category to which they belong:

Group I	Group II
Left hand with extended index finger;	Right hand palm open, turned up in lap;
Harsh, shrill voice;	the words: *I do everything I can to help her; I love her so very much.*
Rapid rate of speech;	
↓	↓
Satir Category 2	Satir Category I
(blaming)	(placating)

The use of these two sorting techniques in conjunction with one another have, in every case in our experience, resulted in a sorting of incongruities into polarities which forms the basis for a profound integration and growth step for the client involved. We have noted over and over again certain patterns in the way that representational systems and Satir category sort out. In the order of their frequency and effectiveness, they occur in the following way:

Representational Systems Polarities

Visual	Kinesthetic
Visual	Auditory
Auditory	Kinesthetic
Kinesthetic	Kinesthetic

Satir Category Polarities

Blaming 2	Placating 1
Blaming 2	Super-reasonable 3
Super-reasonable 3	Placating 1
Placating 1	Placating 1

The interaction of these two principles provides much of the power when they are used in combination. The most useful generalizations from our experience are that the following Satir Categories consistently occur with the representational systems listed:[9]

Representational System | Satir Category

Representational System	Satir Category
Kinesthetic	Placating 1
Visual	Blaming 2
Auditory	Super-reasonable 3

With these correspondences, therapists have an extremely powerful organizing principle in aiding them in sorting incongruities into polarities. Any polarity which displays the postures, gestures and syntax of a Satir Category 1 (placating) (Group II, for example) can be instructed by the therapist in the use of kinesthetic predicates; in the case of a polarity which shows a Satir Category 2 in posture, gestures, etc., the therapist knows to best assist the client in this sorting phase by insuring that he uses predicates which presuppose a visual representational system. In our experience, by far the most frequently occurring combination is a polarity split wherein one polarity is a Satir 1 (placating) with a kinesthetic representational system while the other polarity is a Satir 2 (blaming) with a visual representational system. There is a large amount of information, especially from neurological sources, which indicates that, while a human being has a kinesthetic representational system present in both hemispheres, the two cerebral hemispheres are specialized with respect to the other two representational systems, visual and auditory. Specifically, the language portion of the auditory representational system is localized in the so-called dominant cerebral hemisphere while the visual representational system is localized in the non-dominant cerebral hemisphere.[10] Each of the representational system polarity splits which we have found useful in our work is consistent with the generalization that incongruities can be very effectively sorted into polarities whose representational systems are located in different hemispheres. This helps us to understand the extraordinary power of the combined representational system—Satir Category sorting principle.

We have presented five general techniques which a therapist may use to help the client to sort incongruent paramessages into polarities. The first three of these — spatial sorting, fantasy sorting, and psychodramatic sorting — can easily be used in combination with the last two — representational system and Satir Category sorting. For example, in using a spatial sorting technique, the therapist can apply the representational system and Satir Category sorting principles. The therapist must be alert to watch and to listen, making sure that the spatially sorted polarities have distinct representational systems and distinct Satir Categories. In addition, the first three techniques also can be used in conjunction with one another. For example, when we presented the example of a fantasy sorting technique, we mentioned that it had the advantage of presenting the client with visual and auditory representations of his polarities in a way not available in the spatial sorting technique. However, notice that, in the spatial sorting technique with the two chairs, when the client moved from one chair to the other, the therapist routinely had the client fantasize his other polarity visually and auditorily in the other chair, thereby combining the advantages of the two techniques in a natural way. This is, in fact, a standard procedure for us in teaching people in our Therapist Training Seminars. For us, the most important piece of information with which we present you in this section is that the examples are intended as an initial *guide* for your behavior, and we intend them *only* as a guide. The principle of which they are an example is that of converting a client's simultaneous incongruities into polarities, each congruent in its expression. We encourage you to create new, exciting and original ways of helping clients with this second step — changing their incongruities into resources in their continuing growth as alive human beings.

EXPRESSING POLARITIES

We turn now to the question of specific ways of assisting the client in fully expressing each of his polarities. As mentioned in the example, one excellent way for the therapist to work to accomplish this is for him to act as a movie or play director. In this way, he uses his ability to detect incongruities and to instruct the client in learning to express himself congruently. In doing this, the therapist demands a wholly congruent presentation by the client of each of the polarities. Often the therapist will, himself, demonstrate the congruency of presentation of the polarity which he wants the client to achieve, thus presenting himself as a model for the client. We have discovered a number of other ways of doing this in addition to the movie/play-director technique.

One way of assisting the client in fully expressing each of his polarities is to use the Meta-model techniques detailed in *Magic I*. In this technique, challenging the form of the client's language representation to require that the client fill in any deletion (portions of the sentences which have been left out) and specify verbs (give descriptions of processes which allow both the client himself and the therapist to connect the language representation with the experience), and then using the other Meta-model distinctions allow the therapist a systematic way of completing each of the client's polarities.

In our experience, one of the difficulties in aiding clients in fully expressing each set of paramessages as a congruent polarity is that frequently the client is able to express one of the polarities fully (the more fully expressed polarity) but has great difficulty in fully developing the other polarity (the less strongly expressed polarity). Here we can offer a maneuver which, in each case in our experience, has been effective in assisting the client in fully expressing the weaker polarity. We call this *playing polarity*. We distinguish two versions of the maneuver of playing polarity. The first occurs when the client himself is deliberately instructed by the therapist to continue to play the more fully expressed polarity; in fact, to play this polarity in as exaggerated a form as the ingenuity of the therapist can assist the client in creating. This move on the part of the therapist will inevitably have as its consequence several positive results. First, the therapist is fully accepting and utilizing the client's behavior — he literally tells the client to do what he is, in fact, already doing. Notice that this leaves the client in the position of having two choices:

(a) Accept the therapist's directions to do in an exaggerated form what he is already doing;

(b) Resist the therapist's directions to do in an exaggerated form what he is already doing.

If the client takes choice (a), he is accepting the therapist's directions as legitimate. Here the issue is often characterized as control — a topic dealt with extensively by Haley (see *Strategies of Psychotherapy*). Typically, when the technique of playing polarity is first presented in our Therapist Training Seminars, the participants are concerned with what at first appears to them to be a manipulative technique. Rather than the issue being one of control, we understand this maneuver to be a full utilization of the limits of the client's model of the world in a way which results in allowing the client to come to express and to accept parts of himself which he had previously suppressed. To claim that the issue is one of control is to accept a model of the world in which one human being has the power to control another human being through manipulation. We discussed this extensively in *Magic I* as a case of semantic ill-formedness (see, especially, Chapters 3 and 4). Here we wish simply to point out that characterizing this maneuver as controlling the behavior of the client does not respect the capacity of the client to learn to respond and fails to give him credit for his vast potential to integrate the many parts of himself. One outcome of the client's accepting the therapist's direction to play his more fully expressed polarity in an exaggerated form is that the client will soon flip polarities. In other words, the outcome for a client who is playing his more fully expressed polarity in an exaggerated form is the emergence of the opposite polarity.[11] This general tactic of playing polarity has different names in different forms of psychotherapy. For example, in Gestalt therapy, this is called *making the rounds* (*Gestalt Therapy Now*, J. Fagen [ed.]). The therapist instructs the client in playing his more fully developed polarity with each member of the group until the client flips polarity. In the context of Brief therapy (see, for example, the cases listed in *Change*, Watzlawick, P.; Weakland, J.; and Fisch, R.), this technique is often assigned to the client in the form of homework. Milton Erickson frequently uses this technique as a first step in his work. For example, in working with a client who is obese and states that he wants to lose weight, Erickson, typically, will instruct the client to gain weight. As Erickson points out, this maneuver presupposes that the client has control over his weight; thus his gaining weight is equivalent to his accepting responsibility in an area of his behavior he had previously considered outside of his control (see *Advanced Techniques of Hypnosis and Therapy,* J. Haley [ed.]).

If the client chooses to reject the therapist's directions [take option (b)], then the typical result is that the client will respond by flipping polarities. Thus, whether the client chooses (a) or (b), the less fully expressed polarity will emerge and the process of growth and change is well underway.

The second variation of playing polarity is for the therapist, himself, to play polarity. Again, the object of this move is to assist the client in fully expressing the weaker of two polarities as a step in preparing to integrate them. Again, the same polarity principle applies. Since the therapist wishes to assist the client in developing the *less* fully expressed polarity, the therapist plays the *more* fully expressed polarity. For example, the therapist adopts the body posture, gestures, tonality, rate of speech, characteristic syntax, appropriate representational system predicates, etc. — all of the output systems present in the client's more fully expressed polarity. The critical portion of this maneuver is that the therapist must be more congruent and forceful in presenting the client with his own polarity than the client is in presenting that polarity. In our experience, the result is immediate and dramatic. The client responds by expressing the formerly weaker polarity. The therapist continues to play the first polarity in an exaggerated form until the client is expressing the opposite polarity with equal intensity. Rarely is the client aware (consciously) of this maneuver on the part of the therapist. Furthermore, even in a case in which the client is perfectly aware that the therapist is playing polarity, he will (prior to integration) respond with the opposite polarity if the therapist continues to express the client's stronger polarity.

Now we consider the process by which the therapist knows that the client has succeeded in sorting his polarities in a way which will allow a significant integration. Since the entire purpose of Phase 2 of incongruity work is to change simultaneous incongruities into sequential incongruities, the therapist uses all of his input channels — he uses his body, touching the client, checking for muscle patterns; his eyes, watching carefully all of the paramessages presented by the client's body postures and movements; his ears, listening intently to the tonality, tempo, and representational system predicates — to determine that the client is congruent in his communication as he expresses first one and then the other polarity. Again, there is, to our knowledge, no substitute for a therapist's having a clear set of eyes and ears and a body which he uses to check for congruency in the client. In our Therapist Training Seminars, we have found it useful to instruct therapists in training to make two very specific checks. A client's incongruities will be considered to be adequately sorted for the purposes of beginning integration when all of the following conditions are present:

(1) Each of the polarities has a consistent representational system which is different from that of the other polarity;
(2) Each of the polarities has a consistent Satir Category which is different from that of the other polarity;
(3) The representational system and Satir Category of each polarity matches the correspondences listed:

Representational System	Satir Category
visual	2
kinesthetic	1
auditory	3

When all of these conditions are satisfied, the therapist then moves to the integration of the polarities — Phase 3 of incongruity work.

INCONGRUITIES INTO PARTS (>2)

We are aware of only one technique which has been developed by any therapeutic wizards to sort more than two parts from the incongruencies presented by a client. This is Virginia Satir's *Parts Party.* We both use this in our work and find it an excellent and effective technique.

In a Satir Parts Party, the psychodramatic technique is utilized fully. Using a projective technique (e.g., the names of a number of well-known people, fictional or real, by whom the client feels particularly attracted or repelled, then assigning each of the famous names an adjective which best describes them to the client), the therapist assists the client in selecting and instructing group members to play each of the parts identified. The group members then interact in the context of a party — each of them behaving one-dimensionally. For example, if, in a client's party, some group member has accepted the responsibility for playing a part characterized by the adjective *angry,* then that person (after the client has instructed him in the specifics of how he expresses anger) will present an angry message with every output channel, with every paramessage, in every contact with the other parts. The client is usually placed in a position in which he can see and hear all of the action of the parts. Typically, the client sees and hears acts by his parts which previously had only occurred in his fantasies as well as behavior which he has been aware of in coping with others in his public experience. Usually, after the client has identified (owned) all of his parts, some crisis occurs in the interaction of the parts, mobilizing them. In this crisis, some of the parts transform into other related abilities or resources and all of the parts learn to cooperate with each other. The final portion of the Parts Party consists of the client's accepting each of his parts as a resource — the integration phase.

In assisting the client in identifying with a projective technique the parts or resources which he has, we have found it useful to have the client select an equal number of male and female well-known personages. Often we ask for about half of the number with which we want to work. Once this has happened and the client has assigned adjectives to the people selected, we ask the client to give us an adjective which is the polar opposite for each of the adjectives already chosen, one by one — in effect, an adjective which describes the part of him which is maximally incongruent in his model of the world with the part being described. Using this approach, we identify and simultaneously balance so-called *good* and *bad* parts with respect to the client's model of the world. This corresponds to Phase 1 of the polarity work we have described so far. The portion of the Parts Party in which the client, with the therapist's help, instructs each of the people selected to play the parts is most closely associated with Phase 2 of the polarity work we have been describing. Here, typically, we ask the client to instruct the person playing some particular part, *anger*, for example, by being angry at this point in time. Using guided fantasy or enactment techniques (see *Magic I*, Chapter 6 for a description) we assist the client in literally showing the person who will play the angry part the exact way in which to play it. As the client shows the person how to be angry by being angry, we use our skills in detecting incongruent paramessages to assist the client in being maximally congruent in his expression of anger. Here again the techniques described previously in assisting the client in becoming maximally congruent apply — for example, acting as a movie or play director, checking for consistent representational system predicates, etc. Once the client has expressed his anger part congruently, we ask the person who will play that part to copy all of the paramessages — the body posture, the movements, the tonality. Now we make the client the movie or play director. His task is to mold the person who will play his anger part into the body posture, movements, tonality, etc., which most congruently represent, for him, his anger part.

Once all of the first set of adjectives have been assigned to people and the people have been instructed by the client specifically how to play these parts, we ask the client for the adjective which is the polar opposite of each of these, as mentioned above. Again, we ask the client to assign this new part to some group member. Here we have found it useful, as the client begins to instruct the people who will play each of the polar opposites, for the person who will play the original adjective to come forward and begin to interact with the client. The outcome of this (whether the client is aware of the maneuver or not) is that the client quickly becomes maximally congruent in the expression of the polar opposite, thus providing an excellent model for the person who will play that adjective. Again, the therapist may choose to play the polar adjective himself rather than have the person assigned the adjective come forward and do it. Once the party begins, the client, with the therapist's help, works to make the players maximally congruent in their presentations of the parts they have been assigned.

The same principles which we have presented previously for polarity work apply in the parts party. The strategy for the therapist is to assist the client in sorting his incongruencies into a number of parts. Some of these parts have the polar opposite relationship and, therefore, the therapist makes use of explicit ways of determining whether the polarities are well sorted (e.g., two polar opposites do not share representational systems). The overall task for the therapist in this work is to sort the client's conflicting and simultaneously incongruently expressed models of the world into parts, each of which is congruent. This prepares the stage for Phase 3, Integration, in which the client will be able to use these incongruencies as resources to assist him in coping with the world and in his continuing growth. By this process the therapist helps the client to transform the conflicting parts of himself — parts which previously had been the source of pain and dissatisfaction, parts which had by their antagonism to each other prevented him from getting the things he wanted for himself — into resources which he may now use to create a full, rich, coordinated, and exciting life for himself, the transformation of pain into a basis for growth.

PHASE 3
INTEGRATING THE CLIENT'S INCONGRUITIES

Once the therapist has assisted the client in sorting his incongruities into polarities, the integration phase (Phase 3) begins. Here the overall strategy is for the therapist to help the client to coordinate his polarities so that these polarities become resources for the client rather than the basis of pain and dissatisfaction. Another way of stating this overall strategy is that the therapist works with the client to assist him in achieving *meta-position* with respect to his polarities (or parts, in the case in which more than two of the client's parts are being worked with). A person has achieved meta-position with respect to his polarities (parts) when he has choices in his behavior (whether consciously or not) about whether he will behave in a way which is characteristic of one polarity (part) or the other in a smooth, coordinated fashion, when neither polarity (part) interrupts the other, and the client expresses both polarities appropriately and congruently. We divide the integration phase of incongruency work into two portions — *contact* and *integration*.

CONTACT BETWEEN THE POLARITIES

So far, in the incongruity work the therapist and the client have worked to transform a set of simultaneously presented incongruent paramessages into a series of sequentially presented congruent polarities (parts). These polarities are now sharply distinguished — they have distinct Satir categories and distinct representational systems. In other words, the client has changed from a confused, self-interrupting, tortured, incongruent human being into one who can express himself forcefully and congruently at each point in time. Since these polarities, each congruent, are organized in different representational systems, they have no systematic way of making contact. The therapist has many choices about the way that he helps the client's polarities to make contact. We will now describe some of these choices. However, we first want to remind you that these are only a guide to assist you in your work; we encourage you to develop other methods which you will find useful. The more choices you have as a therapist, the more effective and creative you will be as a people-helper. Secondly, these choices are not mutually exclusive; we encourage you to find combinations of these choices which will make your work more powerful.

Choosing the Representational System for Contact

At this point in therapy, the client's polarities do not have a representational system in common — they, quite literally, have no way of making contact. Here the therapist's fundamental choices are whether to work to give one of the polarities the representational system which the other has, to give each of the polarities the other's representational system, or to introduce a representational system new to *both* of the polarities in which they can make contact. Naturally, the therapist may choose to do all of these so that the outcome is that each of the polarities has all three representational systems, and thus they make contact in all of them.

No matter which of the options the therapist takes at this point in therapy, he will be particularly aware of his use and the client's use of predicates. If, for example, the therapist has decided to begin the contact phase by assisting a visual Satir 2 polarity in developing an ability to represent his experience kinesthetically — to get in touch with his feelings — he will deliberately shift the predicates which he is using from ones such as *see, watch, clear,* — which presuppose a visual representational system — to ones such as *feel, touch, sensitive,* which presuppose a kinesthetic representational system. Furthermore, the therapist will listen carefully to the client's responses to him to determine whether the client shifts to the matching predicates. We present now two examples of a therapist making a choice about representational systems and beginning the process of putting the polarities into contact.

EXAMPLE 1

The therapist has sorted the client's incongruencies into two polarities, using the Perls-type, empty-chair technique. One of the client's polarities is a blaming, visual polarity and the other a placating, kinesthetic one. The client, a woman named Beatrice, is in the visual, blaming polarity chair, congruently expressing her anger.

> *Therapist:* ... Yes, and tell her exactly what you see as you look over there at her, sitting there crying.
> *Beatrice:* Yeah, I know ... I watch you ... you always sit around crying and feeling sorry for yourself. Your eyes are so filled with tears that you can't even see what you're doing.
> *Therapist:* Now, Beatrice, switch to the other chair!
> *Beatrice:* (Moving over to the other chair, her body posture, gestures, tonality shifting to a set of paramessages which are congruently placating) oh ... (crying quietly) ... oh, I

feel so bad . . . my stomach hurts and I just want to be left alone (continuing to cry).

Therapist: (Noting that Beatrice is expressing each of her polarities congruently and that they are sorted so that there is no overlap between representational systems and Satir categories, the therapist decides to use the representational system which neither of the polarities has to assist them in making contact — the auditory system.) Beatrice, did you hear what she (therapist indicating the visual, blaming polarity chair, now empty) said to you?

Beatrice: What? . . . what she said. (looking at the other chair) Yes, I think so. . . .

Therapist: Tell me, what did she say?

Beatrice: . . . oh . . . I'm not sure; I guess I didn't hear her.

Therapist: OK, now, Beatrice, ask her what she said to you. Call her by name.

Beatrice: Beatrice, what did you say to me?

Therapist: Move! (Beatrice moves to the other chair, again her body and other output channels shifting to the blaming polarity.) Now, Beatrice, respond!

Beatrice: Respond? . . . respond to what?

Therapist: Did you hear what she said to you?

Beatrice: . . . Well, no, but she always . . .

Therapist: (Interrupting Beatrice) Ask her what she said!

Beatrice: Well, what did . . . (interrupting herself) oh, I remember.

Therapist: What?

Beatrice: She asked me what I had said to her.

Therapist: Now, respond to her.

Beatrice: All you ever do is sit around and cry and feel sorry for yourself.

Therapist: Beatrice, switch chairs (Beatrice moves). Now did you hear what she said?

Beatrice: Yes, she said that all I ever do is sit around feeling sorry for myself.

Therapist: Yes; now respond.

The therapist continues to work with Beatrice, checking to insure each time that she moves that she accurately heard what the other polarity has said before attempting to respond. In this way, the two polarities begin to make contact with one another, to make their needs known, and to learn to communicate and cooperate with one another so they are truly resources for Beatrice rather than a source of pain and dissatisfaction.

EXAMPLE 2

Mark, a young man in his mid-twenties, a member of one of our Therapist Training Groups, has worked with one of the therapists to sort his incongruencies into a placating, kinesthetic polarity and a blaming, visual polarity. The therapist has decided to work to give each of the polarities the representational system that the other has in order to allow them to make contact.

> *Mark:* (In the kinesthetic, placating position) I just want to feel good, I just want to relax. . . .
>
> *Therapist:* Mark, take a deep breath, sit back and loosen the muscles in your chest and neck, and as you do this, look carefully across in front of you and see what you see sitting in the chair opposite you. (Mark adjusts his body and looks up.) Yes, and what do you see?
>
> *Mark:* . . . Well, it's hard for me to see. I . . . oh, OK, yes, I see a guy standing there pointing his finger at me and he's yelling at me. . . .
>
> *Therapist:* Yes, and how does his face look to you as you watch him doing this?
>
> *Mark:* He looks angry . . . ah . . . tight . . . you know . . . he looks like he's really unhappy about something.
>
> *Therapist:* Now, Mark, switch.
>
> *Mark:* (Moving to visual, blaming chair, shifting his body appropriately) He (pointing to the first chair) really pisses me off . . . he never . . .
>
> *Therapist:* (Interrupting Mark) Mark, as you sit there, looking at him, how do you feel, in your body?
>
> *Mark:* . . . What? . . . feel, in my body?
>
> *Therapist:* Yes Mark, what are you aware of at this point in time, in your body?
>
> *Mark:* . . . Well, I really don't know. . . . I'm not sure what I feel . . .
>
> *Therapist:* Yes; now allow your eyes to close and become aware of your body. (Mark responds) Now, Mark, tell me what you are aware of in your body.
>
> *Mark:* Wow! I'm so tight in my shoulders . . . my stomach feels twisted up . . . my eyes feel hot (and he begins to cry slowly).

The therapist continues to work with Mark, systematically switching predicates and checking to make sure that Mark also shifts predicates, so that Mark now has the ability to see and to feel in both positions. In this way, Mark's polarities begin to make contact, an essential step en route to Mark's achieving meta-position with respect to his polarities.

Fully Expressed Polarities During Contact

Once the therapist has established a representational system in which the client's polarities can make contact, he will work to insure that each polarity expresses itself fully to the other. The most comprehensive way to assist each of the client's polarities to express itself fully verbally is the Meta-model techniques — the subject of *Magic I.* In other words, the therapist checks the client's verbal expressions for the well-formed-in-therapy conditions — all of the statements made by each polarity must contain no deletions, no nominalizations, no unspecified verbs; all nouns must have referential indices, etc. There are two special adjustments to standard Meta-model challenges which we have found useful in the context of polarity work.

First, in standard Meta-model challenges, when a polarity has made a statement which includes a modal operator of necessity or possibility (see *Magic I,* Chapters 3 and 4) as the following sentences do:

> *Client:* I can't accept help.
> *Client:* It's impossible for me to ask for things for myself.

the therapist may challenge by asking:

> *Therapist:* What stops you from accepting help?
> *Therapist:* What stops you from asking for things for yourself?

In the context of polarity work, we suggest that you adjust these challenges to:

> *How does he* (indicating the other polarity) *stop you from accepting help?*
> *How does he* (indicating the other polarity) *stop you from asking for things for yourself?*

Here, the therapist's challenge/question presupposes that the opposite polarity is the thing/person which stops the polarity from getting what it wants. This assists the client in focusing on the process by which the two polarities interrupt and defeat each other, thus serving as the basis for the client's incongruities, pain and dissatisfaction.

The second adjustment to standard Meta-model challenge/ questioning in polarity work is to incorporate the appropriate representational system predicates into the Meta-model challenges. For example, using the same sentences as above:

Client: I can't accept help.
Client: It's impossible for me to ask for things for myself.

the therapist, when working with a visual polarity, may respond by challenging with:

Therapist: What do you see stopping you from accepting help?
Therapist: What do you see stopping you from asking for things for yourself?

By adjusting the Meta-model challenge/questions to include the predicates which match the representational system predicates that the client's polarity uses, the therapist assists the polarity in understanding and responding fully. [12]

Naturally, the therapist may use these two adjustments together — that is, each presupposes that the other polarity is the thing/person which is stopping the first polarity from getting what it wants — and incorporate the appropriate representational system predicates into the Meta-model challenges. For example, using the same client's statements as before:

Client: I can't accept help.
Client: It's impossible for me to ask for things for myself.

the therapist may choose to respond with:

Therapist: How do you see him stopping you from accepting help?
Therapist: How do you see him stopping you from asking for things for yourself?

In addition to Meta-model challenges/questioning, we have developed a set of polarity questions which we have found very useful in assisting polarities in making contact. This set of polarity questions is designed to make sure that each polarity expresses its own needs directly in a form specific enough that both the therapist and the other polarity come to understand what that polarity really wants.

Polarity Questions

What, specifically, do you want for you (feel)

How, specifically, does he (indicating the o you from getting what you want for yourself?

Is there any way that you hear-see-feel tha polarity) can be of any use to you?

What would happen if he (the other polarity) w completely? How would this be of use to you?

Do you see-hear-feel what he (the other polarity) wants?

What would happen if you allowed him (the other polarity) to have what he wants?

Do you see-feel-hear that there is any way that you both (i.e., both polarities) could get what you want?

By asking each polarity this special set of polarity questions, in combination with the standard Meta-model challenges, the therapist insures full expression of each polarity. As a polarity responds to each of these questions, the response will be a set of paramessages which the therapist then checks for congruity. Furthermore, the therapist checks the verbal paramessages against the well-formed-in-therapy conditions.

If the therapist has decided to use the auditory representational system as the one in which the two polarities will make contact, then we suggest that, rather than ask the Meta-model questions and Polarity questions of the polarity, the therapist instruct the one polarity to tell the other polarity what is missing, what he wants.

For example, in place of the following exchanges:

(1) *Client:* I want things for myself.
Therapist: What things, specifically?

(2) *Client:* I can't accept help.
Therapist: How do you see-feel-hear that he (the other polarity) stops you from accepting help?

(3) *Client:* It's impossible for me to ask for things for myself.
Therapist: How do you see-hear-feel he (the other polarity) stops you from asking for things for yourself?

the therapist directs the polarity to talk, not to the therapist, but directly to the other polarity as in the following:

Client: I want something for myself.
Therapist: Tell him what, specifically, you want for yourself.

(2) *Client:* I can't accept help.
Therapist: Tell him how, specifically, you see-hear-feel that he stops you from accepting help.

(3) *Client:* It's impossible for me to ask for things for myself.
Therapist: Tell him how you hear-see-feel that he, specifically, stops you from asking for things for yourself.

In example (1) above, the therapist is developing the client's auditory representational system for the purpose of making contact. It is appropriate in cases such as this to direct the client to answer these polarity questions by instructing him to tell the other polarity the answer. Again, as in example 1, the therapist will check to make sure that the polarity which is to respond has actually heard the question or statement before responding.

Most commonly, in our experience, the systematic application of these contact techniques — the choice of representational system(s), Meta-model challenges/questions (adjusted for polarity work), and the polarity questions — results in the polarities' fully expressing themselves and making an agreement or contract. In our Therapist Training Seminars, we have developed a set of techniques which are useful in making sure that the agreement or contact between polarities is solid enough to lead to full integration of those previously conflicting parts.

Checking for a Solid Contact

Once a client's polarities have each fully expressed itself and they have made contact, the therapist's task is to assist the polarities in reaching an agreement which will allow them to work smoothly with each other, thereby becoming resources for the client. Very often, the polarities once put in touch with one another, will reach a solid contact which will serve as the basis for their coordinated action. When this doesn't occur spontaneously, the therapist may intervene by:

(1) Determining, specifically, where the two polarities come into conflict;
(2) Having them each decide how they can best make use of each other's skills in these areas of behavior in which they had previously been in conflict;

(3) Setting up cues by which each of the polarities can signal the other for assistance under these stress situations.

The systematic use, by the therapist himself, of the contact techniques previously presented will allow him rapidly to find out in what areas of behavior the polarities conflict and also how they can best come to coordinate their efforts. Here, since each of the polarities has some skills which the other does not have (for example, when the polarities are sorted visual/kinesthetic, one polarity can be given the task of paying attention to what can be seen in the stress situation and the other polarity what can be felt), it is largely a matter of assigning each of the polarities tasks consistent with their special skills.

The third step in checking for a solid contact — that of establishing cues — signals between the polarities — requires more comment. When under stress, one of the polarities begins to behave in a way which will bring the two polarities into conflict: it is very useful that the polarities have signals by which one can inform the other that this is happening. Such signals allow the polarities to coordinate their skills in a non-conflicting way. For example, a therapist working with a visual-blaming/kinesthetic-placating polarity sort has the following as a choice in establishing cues:

Therapist: (Talking to Margot's kinesthetic polarity) And what are you aware of at this point in time, Margot?

Margot: Wow; I'm so excited. I understand now how we (the two polarities) can work together. When I start to feel tight and I don't understand what's happening, she (the other polarity) can help me out by looking around and seeing exactly what is going on, so I don't become paralyzed.

Therapist: Yes; now, switch over, Margot. (Margot moves to the other chair.) Now, Margot, what are you aware of?

Margot: I'm really clear about how this will work; I can really see how useful she (the other polarity) can be to me. I hate being numb — having no feeling — so when I see that starting to happen, she can help me not to become numb.

Therapist: (Beginning to set up cue signals) OK; now, the only thing I don't understand yet is how, specifically, you can let her know you need her help?

Margot: . . . What? I don't understand.

Therapist: When you notice that you are beginning to feel numb, how will you let her know you need her help?

Margot: Well, I'm not sure . . .

Therapist: Margot, what's the very first thing that you're aware of when you start to go numb?

Margot: (her breathing reverses) I ... I stop breathing ... , sort of ... like right now — I'm beginning to go numb.

Therapist: All right — now, how about using that very thing as a signal to your other part to help you not to go numb.

Margot: Yes, I think I understand; when I start to reverse my breathing, I'll take a really deep breath and ask my other part for help. ...

ACHIEVING META-POSITION

The last and most important area of working with incongruity is that of assisting the client in achieving meta-position with respect to his polarities. This means that, as a therapist, in order to make your work thorough and lasting, you will be required to do a little more than just put polarities into contact with one another. In order for the client to recode his polarities and sorted para-messages in such a way as to allow permanent change and there-fore, true meta-position, sustained contact and integration may be required, although not always.

Once the polarities have a well-formed sort, maximal separa-tion, and then contact in the same representational system, you, as a therapist, are prepared for integration. To achieve integration and, therefore, meta-position, your client's two or more sets of representations which have been put into contact in the same representational system must now be given the impetus to re-organize themselves into a new, single representation which will include all of the paramessages of both and will be itself greater than the sum of the two. For example: If a client has two polarities (A and B), where A implied not B and B implied not A, they are a mutually exclusive representation for the same terri-tory. Meta-position would not be a representation of A plus B but rather a set of plus or minus (AB) equaling some representation (X) that had all the potentials of A and B as well as Not A and Not B and the rich choices that result from many combinations within and between the polarities.

Consider the following example of Dennis, who presented the therapist with a highly incongruent communication about his interaction with others in the world, simply stating that he wishes others to like him. The polarities which were sorted out of this communication were a kinesthetic-placating part which felt he must do what others expected of him or he wasn't a good person and no one would like him, along with a visual blaming part which saw other people pushing him around, being cruel to him and undeserving of his kindness. These two representations were conflicting maps for the same territory and the result was a deadlock in his behavior, kind words with a grating tonality. His polarities were put into contact in his visual representational system (fantasy, mind's eyes) by having him create two images of himself, standing side by side, one the part which Dennis felt must placate others, the other the part of Dennis which saw how people abused him. He was told to watch these two argue and report on their interaction, both visually as well as auditorily. The result was that Dennis was simultaneously representing both his polarities, visual and auditory, from the perspective of an observer.

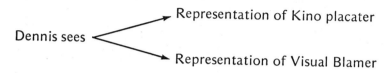

Although simultaneous representation had been achieved in the same representational system, along with contact, meta-position had not yet been fully achieved. Dennis was asked to comment on the assets of both polarities and then asked if he would try something which might be new to him. His response was affirmative. He was then told:

Dennis, now, as you continue to sit there with your eyes closed, I would like you to gently reach up with both hands, grasping these two images, one in each hand. That's right (Dennis reaches up). Now, slowly push these two together, together into one image, watching closely, seeing how both change into one. (Dennis pushes them together slowly, gasping as his hands approach each other.) Now, what do you see?

Dennis: It's me, but different.
Therapist: How?
Dennis: I look strong, but not mean.
Therapist: Anything else?
Dennis: Yes; he can be gentle and care about people and . . . yes, he's not weak and mushy either.
Therapist: You see a picture of yourself having all of those qualities at the same time?
Dennis: Yes (sighing).
Therapist: Do you like what you see?
Dennis: Yes.
Therapist: Would you like to make that a part of yourself, and

have those abilities as your resources?

Dennis: Sure.

Therapist: Good. Then, continuing to hold this image of yourself gently and watching it carefully, slowly pull the image
into yourself. That's right. (Dennis pulls his hands slowly
toward his body.) Now, let this come inside, become a part
of you, a resource all the way inside of you. (Dennis places
his hands against his body, breathing deeply. As he does,
his face flushes with color and he sighs loudly.)

Therapist: How do you feel as this becomes a part of you?

Dennis: All tingly in my chest.

Therapist: Let it spread all through your body as this becomes
truly a part of you.

Through this process, Dennis achieves meta-position, recoding
his polarities visually into a single representation. The therapist
tested his work by playing Dennis' polarities but Dennis was no
longer incongruent in this way; he only laughed where before he flew
into anger. His softened facial muscles and laughter were sure signs
of achieving meta-position and integration of this set of polarities.

Recoding of polarities can be accomplished in any representational system by representing the polarities simultaneously and
then arranging for a single representation. Even in the case of the
Parts Party described earlier, the paramessages which are represented by different people are, at the end of the Parts Party,
unified into a single group. Then a short ritual is performed which
results in simultaneous repression kinesthetically by having the
client stand in the middle of a circle of the people who are playing
his parts and each part lays a hand on the client, stating the ability
he represents, until the client has hands from each part touching
him simultaneously and has stated his acceptance congruently.

So, the resulting strategy for integration of polarities is first,
contact in the same representational system and then, secondly,
recoding into a single representation. Thus meta-position and
integration are achieved.

META-TACTICS FOR INCONGRUITY

When a human being is incongruent in his behavior, he is
signaling that he has more than one model of his world. This is an
important piece of information for the therapist. The immediate
acceptance and use of the client's incongruity as a basis for growth
and change in the ways desired by the client are powerful therapeutic tools. Since incongruent paramessages are signals of the
presence in the client of conflicting models of the world, the

overall task of the therapist is to assist the client in creating a new model of the world in which the two formerly conflicting models will operate in a coordinated, smooth way, allowing the client all of the choices available in both of the previous models. In other words, the therapist works to assist the client in achieving meta-position — that is, in creating a map of the world for his behavior which includes both of the models previously in conflict. In this way, the client comes to have the choice he desires in that area of his behavior.

The process of assisting the client in achieving meta-position can be broken down into three phases to assist you in organizing your experience:

(1) Identifying incongruity (conflicting paramessages);
(2) Sorting the paramessages;
(3) Integration of the sorted paramessages.

Another way of representing the process of a therapist's assisting the client in achieving meta-position is in terms of the changes in the client's communication behavior over time. Again, we have found it useful in our Therapist Training Seminars to distinguish three phases of this process:

(1) The client's communication is incongruent — he is attempting to present paramessages from more than one non-compatible model of the world *simultaneously;*
(2) The client's communication is congruent at each point in time and incongruent over time — here he attempts to present paramessages from more than one non-compatible model of the world *sequentially;*
(3) The client's communication is congruent *both simultaneously and sequentially.* He has achieved meta-position, and has a unified, coordinated map for his behavior.

The process of achieving meta-position is, then, the overall strategy for working with clients' incongruities, thereby transforming the source of their pain and paralysis into a resource for growth, energy and vitality. Accepting this breakdown of the process of achieving meta-position into the three phases, we will present the Meta-Tactics for working with incongruity by phase.

META-TACTICS FOR PHASE 1

In Phase 1, the therapist's task is to *identify* incongruity in the client's communication. The Meta-Tactics for Phase 1, then, are:

Meta-Tactic 1 for Phase 1 (Incongruity):
Compare Paramessages

Here the therapist makes use of all of his input channels, distinguishing what he sees, from what he hears, from what he feels. By first distinguishing the information reaching him through each of his input channels, the therapist accomplishes several things. He is able to avoid becoming incongruent in his own communication in response to the client's incongruity. He avoids becoming depressed, burdened, weighed down (common results of see-feeling and hear-feeling incongruent communication), leaving him free to act creatively. Furthermore, by making these distinctions, he has the basis for comparing the paramessages the client is presenting to check for incongruity in the communication.

Meta-Tactic 2 for Phase 1 (Incongruity):
But

Often the client will make statements to the therapist in which he claims to want something for himself. Statements which have the general form:

$$I \begin{Bmatrix} \text{want} \\ \text{need} \\ \text{would like to} \end{Bmatrix} \begin{Bmatrix} \text{have} \\ \text{do} \end{Bmatrix} X.$$

The therapist may accelerate the process of identifying the incongruencies in the client when he hears statements of this form by leaning forward and saying:

... *but* ...

The client will continue the statement he originally started, filling in the second half of the sentence (the part which follows the word *but*). The verbal material he provides can be used by the therapist in ways which we presented in detail in *Magic I*. The important piece in this context is that, as he completes the sentence, the client's paramessages will shift radically compared with the paramessages which he presented in the first part of the sentence, thus providing the therapist with a set of conflicting paramessages from which change can begin.

Meta-Tactic 3 for Phase 1 (Incongruity).
Meta-Question

The use of this tactic typically occurs when the client has just expressed some powerful feeling he has about some portion of his experience. For example:

I'm really angry about the way she ignores what I say!

At this point the therapist leans forward and says:

. . . and how do you feel about feeling angry about that?

The client's response to this question provides verbal material subject to the Meta-model well-formed-in-therapy conditions. More important for the purposes of the present discussion, the set of paramessages which the client displays when responding to this question can be compared for incongruities with the set he presented when making the original statement.

Meta-Tactic 4 for Phase 1 (Incongruity):
Left-Right Paramessage Check

One abundant source for recognizing incongruity in a client's communication comes from the fact that the two cerebral hemispheres in human brains control the two (opposite) sides of the person's body. The therapist will find that, by visually checking the client's face (e.g., eye size and location on the side of the face, lip form, muscle tones, etc.), hand position and movements, he will discover differences in the paramessages being expressed. The therapist may check auditorily for tone versus syntax in the client's speech. Again, these differences provide the therapist with ways of identifying incongruity.

The four Meta-Tactics for Phase 1 are not intended to present all of the techniques available to each of you as a therapist in your people-helping work; rather, we hope that they will provide you with a take-off point from which you may generate your own modes of working quickly and effectively with the people who come to you for assistance in gaining new choices and energy in their lives.

META-TACTICS FOR PHASE 2

In Phase 2, the therapist's task is to sort the conflicting paramessages which the client has presented to him into fully expressed, congruent parts or polarities. In other words, the simultaneously expressed conflicting models which he identified in the client's communication must be converted into two (or n, in the case of parts) fully represented parts expressed congruently simultaneously and incongruent sequentially.

Meta-Tactic 1 for Phase 2 (Incongruity): Movie/Play Director

Here the therapist uses all of his input channels to represent the paramessages the client is presenting — he works as a movie or play director to get the most convincing "performance" from the client: the performance in which all of the client's output channels are expressing the same or consistent paramessages.

Meta-Tactic 2 for Phase 2 (Incongruity): Spatial Sorting

Having identified the polarities which are the expression of the client's inconsistent models of the world, the therapist locates one of the polarities in one chair and the other in another chair. This assists both the client and the therapist in separating the behavior appropriate for the differing parts of the client.

Meta-Tactic 3 for Phase 2 (Incongruity): Fantasy Sorting

Typically, the therapist makes use of the technique of Guided Fantasy (see *Magic I*, Chapter 6) to assist the client in fully expressing his polarities. By having the client describe the fantasized visual representation of each of his polarities in turn, the therapist has the opportunity to check the described characteristics of the image as well as the paramessages which the client is presenting as he describes his fantasy.

Meta-Tactic 4 for Phase 2 (Incongruity): Psychodramatic Sorting

After the therapist has identified the polarities with which he intends to work, he selects two members of the group to play these polarities; that is, each of these group members adopts all of the paramessages which are congruent for the polarity which he is representing. Usually, the therapist will have the client act as the movie/play director, instructing each of the group members on how to play his part most convincingly (congruently).

Meta-Tactic 5 for Phase 2 (Incongruity):
Representational System Sorting

The therapist listens for predicates which identify different representational systems as the client sequentially expresses each of the polarities. By systematically changing his own predicates as the client expresses each of his polarities, the therapist can accelerate the separation of the polarities into distinct representational systems — one of the conditions for a well-formed sort prior to beginning the integration phase.

Meta-Tactic 6 for Phase 2 (Incongruity):
Satir Category Sorting

The therapist checks to insure that the Satir category of each of the client's polarities is distinct. Non-overlapping of the Satir categories is another of the characteristics of a well-formed sort prior to integration.

Again, in presenting these Meta-Tactics for Phase 2, we have not attempted to list all of the techniques which we have found useful and effective in assisting our clients to break impasses in their behavior. We encourage you to develop ones in addition to those we have presented.

There is one other way of using the Meta-Tactic principles for this phase which has been of great value to us in our work. If you consider the outcome of each of the first four Meta-Tactics for this phase, they sort the client into two separate, congruent polarities. The final two Meta-Tactics can be considered conditions on the two polarities sorted by the first four Tactics and must be considered in relation to each other (e.g., blaming and visual, and not blaming and kinesthetic). Together, these identify the two conditions which are sufficient to allow the client to achieve meta-position through integration. Specifically, the therapist knows that Phase 2 is complete whenever these two conditions are present in the client's communication — that is, when each of the client's polarities are:

(1) Congruently expressed sequentially;
(2) The representational system/Satir category sort meets the well-formedness conditions:

Representational System	Satir Category
visual	blaming 2
kinesthetic	placating 1
auditory	super-reasonable 3

META-TACTICS FOR PHASE 3

In Phase 3 the therapist works to assist the client in converting sequentially incongruent polarities into a single, unified model which allows the client all of the choices he desires in that area of his behavior. It is in this phase that the client achieves meta-position for himself.

Meta-Tactic 1 for Phase 3 (Incongruity):
Contact

Here the therapist works to bring the two fully expressed, congruent and well-sorted polarities into contact with one another. First, since one of the conditions for a well-formed sort in Phase 2 was that the polarities have distinct representational systems, the therapist will select a representational system(s) in which the client can have his polarities make contact.

Secondly, for the client's polarities to make contact, they must be represented simultaneously. Here the choice of sorting which the therapist made in Phase 2 will have an effect. If he had selected a psychodramatic sort, then the contact can take place in either the auditory or visual representational systems, for example. If he had chosen not to use other people (a spatial sort, for example), the auditory representational system, since it is sequential, would not be a good choice, while the visual (fantasized, internal visual images) would. This second condition — simultaneity — is relative to the unit of measurement of time involved. No doubt, at some future date neurological research will become available to specify what the optimum time is in terms of refractory periods. In Perls' polarity work, he sometimes assisted a client in integrating by having him move rapidly from chair to chair — that is, rapidly alternating polarities. The limiting case of this technique is, of course, a simultaneous representation.

Meta-Tactic 2 for Phase 3 (Incongruity):
Re-coding

Once the client's polarities have made contact by a simultaneous, same representational system(s) typical of his polarities, the therapist works to assist him in re-coding the two distinct representations into one. Here, the special set of polarity questions, integration of fantasized visual representations, are useful. The specific ways of re-coding which the therapist may have the client employ are as varied as his ability to be creative will produce. The formal characteristic which they share is the creation by the client through this experience of a single, unified map for his behavior, allowing him the choices he desires from each of the formerly conflicting polarities.

We hope that the partial list of Meta-Tactics to be employed in transforming the client's incongruities from a source of pain, dissatisfaction and paralysis into the basis of growth, energy and change will encourage each of you, as you work in your capacity as a people-helper, to develop additional satisfying Meta-Tactics which are congruent with your own special styles, skills and resources.

FOOTNOTES FOR PART II

1. Perhaps you can identify this pattern from childhood experiences in which the frustrated parent screams at the child to lower his voice — the message here is:

Do what I say, not what I do!

2. The number of output channels and, therefore, messages carried by output channels will vary from client to client. Theoretically, the number of muscle groups which can be independently controlled by the client will determine the number of messages which it is possible for that person to communicate simultaneously. In our experience, it is not necessary for the therapist to attempt to check each of these; rather, we have developed specific ways of checking for match or mismatch among certain groups of these output channels, making use, for example, of the neurological organization common to all humans such as cerebral control of the contralateral side of the body. These principles will be presented later in this part of the book.

3. This seems to us to be more in the spirit of Russell's work. In order for an item to be meta to some other item — for example, the set of all sets is meta to the set of all chairs as it includes the latter as a member but not vice versa — it is necessary for the meta item to include the item it is meta to in its domain. But for a set of simultaneously generated paramessages, no one of them includes any of the others in any sense of *include* that we have found enlightening in organizing our experience in therapy. Russell's statements regarding the Theory of Logical Types can be found in Volume I, Introduction, Chapters 11, 12 and 20; and Volume II, Prefatory Statement of *Principia Mathematica,* and in the American Journal of Mathematics, Volume XXX, 1908, pp. 222-262.

4. Logically, since a representational system may and, in fact, does contain more than one message at a time, it is possible that a message and one of its metamessages may be represented simultaneously. However, since we,

as therapists, can only come to know what messages are represented in a person's representational system through that person's output channels which are limited to one message at a time, this, apparently, has no consequences for communication and therapy.

5. By fully accepting all of the client's behavior, the therapist avoids the phenomenon of "resistance" in his clients and makes full use of the client's skills in assisting in the process of change for that client. We recommend to you the excellent work of Milton H. Erickson, M.D., for examples of utilization of all of the client's behavior (*Advanced Techniques of Hypnosis and Therapy* by J. Haley [ed.], Grune and Stratton, 1967; *Patterns of the Hypnotic Techniques of Milton H. Erickson, M.D.* by R. Bandler and J. Grinder, Meta-Publications, 1975).

6. We present a more detailed and refined model for identifying and utilizing behavior in clients based on the cerebral assymmetries in *Patterns of the Hypnotic Techniques of Milton H. Erickson, M.D.*, by R. Bandler and J. Grinder, Meta-Publications, 1975. This is one of the areas of direct cross-over between psychotherapy and hypnosis.

7. By carefully observing the client as he creates the image, the therapist will have an excellent source of suggestions to the client of what to incorporate into his image — so if the client is biting his lip as he forms this image and biting his lip is a paramessage which is congruent with the paramessages already in the image, then the therapist need only suggest the paramessage of biting his lip as a way in assisting the client in constructing a congruent, fantasized polarity.

8. Notice that, in the example given, the client does not have the accompanying kinesthetic presentations of his polarities. We have noticed that, when creating visual and auditory fantasies, clients often change their body postures and gestures to match those described in the fantasized representation of themselves. Our decision has been to discourage this; we will describe the basis for this decision in Part III, Fuzzy Functions.

9. Satir Category 4 — irrelevant — is usually a rapid sequence of the other Satir categories with the person communicating incongruently both simultaneously and sequentially. Thus, the Satir Category 4 is not useful as a principle for sorting incongruities into polarities as it is itself incongruent.

10. We especially recommend to you the collection of articles, edited by Dimond and Beaumont, in *Hemispheric Functions in the Human Brain*, 1974, John Wiley and Sons, N.Y.

11. We use the term *opposite polarity* to identify the set of paramessages which constitute the client's models of the world which is maximally conflicting with the original polarity. Which set of paramessages constitutes the polar opposite for any particular polarity will differ with each person, for each model of the world. The ways in which polarities flip are an important indicator of the way a client models the world. We will return to this question in a later work.

12. Generalize to all Meta-model challenges.

PART III

Fuzzy Functions

We would like to focus your attention in this section on what we consider to be one of the most important aspects of the Meta-model presented in *Magic I:* semantic well-formedness. Two major forms that semantic well-formedness has as expressed in *Magic I* are:

> Cause-effect
>> *George forced Mary to weigh forty pounds.*
>> *You make me angry.*
>> *She makes me feel depressed.*
> Mind-reading
>> *I know what you're thinking.*
>> *She doesn't like me.*
>> *Everyone hates me.*
>> *He thinks I'm ugly.*

To refresh your memory, we will briefly review these forms.

Cause-Effect semantic ill-formedness is the case in which the referential index of responsibility is placed outside the speaker.

> *You make me angry.*

The speaker, *X*, has no choice about being angry because *Y* forced him to be. Thus, a statement such as:

> *Y Causative verb X feel some emotion*

is said to be semantically ill-formed. Sentences of this type, in fact, identify situations wherein one person does some act and a second person *responds* by feeling a certain way. The point here is that, although the two events occur one after another, there is no necessary connection between the act of the first person and the response of the other. Therefore, sentences of this type identify a model in which the client assigns responsibility for his emotions to people or forces outside his control. The act itself does not cause the emotion; rather, the emotion is a response generated from a model in which the client takes no responsibility for experiences which he could control.

The therapist's task at this point is to challenge the model in some way which will assist the client in taking responsibility for his responses.

We intend in the following pages to more thoroughly explore this phenomenon by examining the experiences which, typically, are the basis for this form of representation.

Mind Reading is any case in which one person, *X*, claims to know the thoughts and emotions of another person, *Y*.

> *I know she is unhappy.*

is an example of this.

The Meta-model challenge for both of these types of semantic ill-formedness can best be summed up by the process question *how*. In Chapter 3 of *Magic I* we described the therapeutic task of dealing with semantic ill-formedness cause-effect as follows:

> *Client's statement*
> (a) My husband makes me mad.
> (b) My husband is unhappy.

The task of helping a client to represent semantically ill-formed representations has two very important dimensions. First, understanding how semantically ill-formed representations are created, and, second, learning to assist the clients in changing the process by which they create semantically ill-formed representations.

SEMANTIC ILL-FORMEDNESS AND FUZZY FUNCTIONS: CAUSE-EFFECT

Numerous child psychologists have made the point that children fail to differentiate themselves from the world around them. They have developed no mechanism either to delete incoming stimuli or even to tell the difference between stimuli originating in the outside world and those originating in their own bodies. The sensory stimuli from each of the input channels in the new infant is represented kinesthetically. For example, if you make a loud noise near a child, the child will cry, not only as a result of the noise, but also by representing the noise as a body sensation. (The child, as well as many adults, will flinch.) The child's major process of representation, then, is to take information from all of his input channels and represent these sensory informations as body sensations. The child *sees* you smile and *feels* good, the child *sees* you sneer and *feels* bad. A stranger smiles and places his huge face in front of a baby; the baby feels frightened and cries.

Thus, we define a fuzzy function as any modeling involving a representational system and either an input channel or an output channel in which the input or output channel involved is in a different modality from the representational system with which it is being used. In traditional psychophysics, this term, *fuzzy function,* is most closely translated by the term *synesthesia.* As we will state throughout this section, fuzzy functions are not bad, crazy or evil, and the outcome of what we consider effective therapy is not the elimination of these functions, but rather the realization that these functions can be the basis for much creative activity on the part of humans as well as being the basis for much suffering and pain. The effective therapeutic outcome, in our experience, is for the client to have a choice as to whether he operates with *fuzzy* functions or with *unfuzzy* functions.

There are two major things to be learned from this as a therapist. First, that many of the so-called imprint experiences which occur in young children are the result of parents and other people failing to respect these see-feel, hear-feel, and feel-feel processes in a young child which may result, although not intended by the adult, in frightening and traumatic experiences for children. The second thing we can learn from this is that we are wired for see-feel, hear-feel representations as children. These circuits do not dissolve as we become adults. Many adults are using these processes of representation when they *see* blood and *feel* sick; they *hear* a yelling, blaming voice and *feel* scared. These processes are particularly common in times of stress. Stress, by its very definition, is a body sensation resulting from some set of events, originating either inside or outside the organism. We are not proposing that this form of representation is bad, wrong, or not useful. We are, rather, pointing out a very frequently occurring part of everyone's stress experiences. When a client says a semantically ill-formed statement such as:

> *My father makes me feel angry.*

we respond by asking how, specifically, he does this. Our client's response will almost inevitably be a description of something he saw or heard (or both) which originated with the father. The client who says semantically ill-formed statements of this Cause-Effect form are either see-feeling, hear-feeling, or both. So, when the above client describes the representation of his experience as:

> *When my father looks at me this way,* (making a face) *I feel angry.*

he is, in fact, describing the experience of see-feeling. Thus, when we say in the above quote from *Magic I* that the client's response is generated from his model of the world, that the resulting emotion felt is a response based on that client's model, and that in a Cause-Effect representation, the referential index of responsibility is being placed upon the world, we are, in fact, describing the result of uncontrolled see-feel and hear-feel circuits. When we say that these clients are taking no responsibility for emotions which they could control, we are not suggesting that everyone should always be reasonable and rational, but, rather, that human beings can have choices about when and where they use the processes of see-feel and hear-feel.[2]

SEMANTIC ILL-FORMEDNESS AND FUZZY FUNCTIONS: MIND-READING

Mind Reading is frequently the result of reversing the process of Cause Effect semantic ill-formedness. In Cause-Effect semantic ill-formedness, the client takes in information through visual and auditory channels and represents that information as a body sensation — a kinesthetic representation. What we have found in the case of Mind Reading is that the client takes body sensations — his kinesthetic representation — and distorts the information arriving visually and auditorially from outside him in such a way that it conforms to his body sensations. For example, a client is depressed and feels worthless in his ongoing relationship with the person he cares about. This other person, totally unaware of the feelings of the first person, arrives home very tired from a day's work. She walks into the room where the client is, waves faintly and groans. The client, using the feelings of depression and worthlessness, interprets the faint wave and groan as a response to his friend's catching sight of him, sitting in the room, turns to the therapist and says:

> *You see, I told you that she thinks that I'm worthless. You heard her groan.*

What has happened here is that the client is reading his friend's mind — he is interpreting (or in more classical psychological terms, projecting) certain analogical communications by his friend (faint wave and a groan) as visual and auditory information that his friend thinks that he is worthless, because that is what he is feeling. The client, then, distorts the visual and auditory information which he receives to make it consistent with his feelings. The way in which each of us distorts the information which we receive visually and auditorially is not random; rather, it is distorted in such a way as to make it maximally consistent with the way that we feel about ourselves at that point in time. In other words, we are exercising our feel-see and feel-hear circuits.[3]

MINI — SO WHAT!

The human beings who come to us, as therapists, seeking our help with pain in their lives, may be at the mercy of see-feel, hear-feel, or other fuzzy-function circuits. Semantic ill-formedness is the result of these fuzzy functions.

$$Cause\text{-}Effect \quad = \quad see\text{-}hear \text{ or } hear\text{-}feel$$
$$Mind\text{-}Reading \quad = \quad feel\text{-}see \text{ or } feel\text{-}hear$$

Or, representing these two processes visually, we have:

Semantic Ill-Formedness

Cause-Effect	*Mind Reading*
Client's Visual and Auditory Input Channels	Client's Visual and Auditory Input Channels
↓	↑
Client's Kinesthetic Representational System	Client's Kinesthetic Representational System

Notice that the result of uncontrolled fuzzy functions associated with Cause-Effect semantic ill-formedness is that, first, the client, literally, has no choice over the way that he feels, and, secondly, he loses touch with (literally) his own ongoing kinesthetic experience as the information which he is receiving visually and auditorially is the basis for his feelings, not what he is presently experiencing kinesthetically. On the other hand, the result of uncontrolled fuzzy functions associated with Mind Reading is that the client distorts his input channels — sets up forward feedback or feed-forward as discussed in *Magic I* — in such a way that he becomes trapped in self-fulfilling prophecies which make change very difficult and rob him of the ability to directly experience the world and his friends.

Many of the therapists we have trained in recognizing this phenomenon have doubted this even more than the identification of representational systems by natural language predicates. We turn now to the work of Paul Bach-y-Rita to show you that, not only do these fuzzy-function circuits exist, but that they can be a great asset as well as the basis of semantically ill-formed representations.

Bach-y-Rita's work is in the area of sensory substitution. He and his co-workers have developed a machine which translates visual input into kinesthetic sensations for the purpose of making it possible for the blind to have some of the resources of the sighted. Blind people trained in use of this machine (the TVSS) can secure information available to the sighted with skill and proficiency. Bach-y-Rita's project has also created another machine which translates auditory input into kinesthetic sensations. He describes, not only the success of his project, but also its neurological foundations in his book, *Brain Mechanism in Sensory Substitution* (1965). He states the following findings from his own work and that of others.

> Indeed, visual responses have been reported to appear earlier in the somesthetic cortex (kinesthetic) than in the specific visual cortex (Kreindler, Crighel, Stoica, and Sotirescu, 1963). Similarly, responses to stimulation of the skin can be recorded from widely varying regions of the cortex, including "specific" somatosensory cortex, associations areas, and even the visual cortex (Murata, Cramer, and Bach-y-Rita, 1965).
>
> In a study of the cat's primary visual cortical cells, Murata, et al., (1965) demonstrated that even these cells were polysensory, with approximately 37% of them responding to auditory and 46% to skin stimulation, compared to the 70% responding to the visual stimulus we employed. Most of the units responding to visual and auditory stimuli also responded to the skin stimulation. . . . These results demonstrated that the visual cortex (the cortex considered most highly specialized of the sensory projection areas) receives input from other sensory modalities as well as visual input, and this suggests an associative or integrating role of at least some cells in this area.

Bach-y-Rita not only demonstrates the existence of cross-over wiring, but finds ways of utilizing these circuits for both the blind and the deaf. The relevance of these circuits to psychotherapy may not yet be evident to the reader, so let us return to the discussion of semantic ill-formedness.

When a therapist uses guided fantasy techniques, that is, when he asks clients to close their eyes and make pictures in their minds of what the therapist describes, the therapist is, in fact, asking the client to use a fuzzy function, viz., to take words (auditory) as input and create visual representations. When a primarily visual client utters the response,

I see what you are saying.

very often they are, literally, making a picture of the therapist's words. As we mentioned in Part I, this is something you can check simply by asking your clients and friends about it when they say such things. These also are fuzzy functions. The term *fuzzy function* was assigned to this type of activity, not because it is a bad activity — in fact, it may be a fantastic resource, as shown by Bach-y-Rita and by the use of guided fantasy in therapy — rather, the phrase, *Fuzzy Function,* was assigned to this particular modeling because so many people lack both a consciousness of this phenomenon and the resulting control over the use of these ways of creating representations. So very often, we have heard people criticize each other for not having the same fuzzy function as they have. For example, when the authors were lecturing at a college, just prior to the beginning of the class, we walked into a heated argument in which one student was criticizing her boyfriend for not being a feeling person. She described him as being insensitive, for not feeling bad when dissecting a dead cat in his biology class (he was not see-feeling). He, in return, described her as being just as insensitive for not feeling sympathy when he told her how he felt about her accusation (she was not hear-feeling). This inter-personal conflict became the focus of our lecture-demonstration until both parties came to understand that neither of their maps was *the right way* of representing reality but each was, in fact, composed of the very differences which we can come to accept and appreciate in other human beings. Also, each of these two students learned something new of the choices which were available to them in the way they represent their world. We helped this woman to learn to see-see as well as see-feel, so she had the choice of taking and passing the biology course as well as many other tasks which would otherwise be painful if she permitted herself only the choice of see-feeling. Many of the people in our Therapist Training Seminars have come to appreciate the skills and choices available to them when they *learn* to use all of their input channels and representational systems in many ways. For instance, many therapists feel great pain as they listen to the problems and trials of their clients. This is not, in itself, a liability; in fact, it can be an asset. However, some of the therapists who have come to us for training have described a feeling of being overwhelmed with the pain of their clients to the extent that they could not really help them. When see-feel and hear-feel circuits go unchecked, and when a client or a therapist finds himself without other choices, the results can be devastating. We believe these may even result in what is commonly called psychosomatic diseases.

We plan in the future to investigate which distinctions of each sensory system (for example, for sight, color, shape, intensity, etc.) can be mapped into which representational system and what the resulting outcomes are, both behavioristically and psychically. We believe that certain combinations of fuzzy functions, if rigidly used, will result in specific psychosomatic diseases. For now, we will return to the application for therapy.

The importance of understanding and working with fuzzy functions cannot be over-emphasized. When therapists first come into contact with this way of describing human behavior, their reaction is often one of, "Well, what does it get me. How can I use it?" There are a number of ways to respond to this question. The first is to understand that people who come for therapy are not (as we said in *Magic I*) bad, sick, crazy, or evil, but are making the best choices available in their model of the world. Take, for example, Martha. She is a young woman about 28 years old who had been convicted of child beating. She had not only been subjected to the ridicule of the courts, her parents, and friends, but, more importantly, ridicule of herself by herself. She had been "treated by several clinicians," and "counseled by her clerical leader." Yet, she still did not trust herself or even like herself. She showed up one evening at a seminar conducted by the authors; she was uninvited and embarrassed, but mostly sorely in need of help. When we inquired about her presence, she apologized and said she would leave. Both authors asked almost simultaneously what she wanted. She immediately began to cry and started to tell her tale. She told of a young marriage and an early divorce, a young child, a boy, whom, though she loved him dearly, she had beaten until she had turned herself over to the authorities, only to lose her son and be "rightfully punished." As she put it,

> *I feel I'm at the end of my rope. I see there is no way for me to feel differently. I just lose control and I can't stop myself. I can't see any way I could feel differently. Sometimes, when I would see my son, I would feel so proud, but when he would do the smallest thing wrong, I felt so*

*mad I'd begin to scold him and something in the way he
looked at me — I just don't know — I'd get madder and
madder until I hit him, and then. . . . I just don't know
what happened. I'd lose control and hit him more and
more — it was like I'd go crazy.*

The authors immediately recognized some patterns which were
familiar to us, even though we had never before worked with a
woman who beat her child. We heard an unusual use of predicates.

I can't see *any way I could* feel *differently.*

This is one of the most direct examples of see-feel predicates we
had encountered. She also made statements such as:

My son looked *warm.*
The judge appeared *to be a* cold *man.*
I can't see *how to grasp my problems.*
Clearly, *this has been* hard *on me.*

All of the above statements are cross-over predicates which presuppose visual input represented kinesthetically. This woman was
a see-feeler. We began, at this point, to explore her model of the
world, using the Meta-model. We were watching and listening to
discover how this woman's see-feeling fuzzy function could result
in child-beating when so many other people's did not. The process
by which this occurred unfolded as we elicited a full representation or model of her experience. The important parameters of
which we became aware (in terms of the information thus far
presented in this volume and in Volume 1) were as follows.
This woman's primary input channel was visual; in fact, she
had very great difficulty communicating as she did not hear many
of our questions and would ask us to repeat them many times. She
could easily understand our questions only if they were phrased in
kinesthetic predicates; her primary representational system was
kinesthetic. She spent most of her time *placating,* and used many
nominalizations in her language communication. Her primary
output channel for communication appeared also to be *kinesthetic;* she communicated by gesture smoothly, nearly always
responding to us by using different facial expressions, smiling or
frowning when we asked how she felt about something. Her verbal
responses were said with a grating tone, and she responded with
words only when we would prod her for verbal answers. When we
asked her to describe again how she came to beat her son, she

described his actions as being much the same as hers (although he was not present to verify this).

So the question of how this young woman suddenly turned into a child beater was still unanswered. Yet, we did know information which could be represented in the following manner:

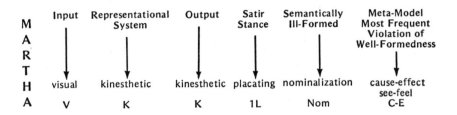

	Input	Representational System	Output	Satir Stance	Semantically Ill-Formed	Meta-Model Most Frequent Violation of Well-Formedness
M A R T H A	visual	kinesthetic	kinesthetic	placating	nominalization	cause-effect see-feel
	V	K	K	1L	Nom	C-E

Visual input is represented as body sensations — nominalized see-feeling which is expressed as placating kinesthetically. We then began to understand the process by which this woman became violent. If you think back to the section on playing polarities, you'll remember that playing a polarity elicits the unplayed polarity, which for this woman was blaming and was still expressed kinesthetically (generally, the polarity of placating is blaming). Furthermore, blaming kinesthetically in its most exaggerated form is violence. One of the authors played the polarity which Martha was playing; he began more congruently than she, matching her voice tone, which she seemed not to notice. He then copied her placating posture, asking in her own tone for her not to be so hard on herself. She did not seem to hear the author's tonality, but, looking intently at him, she first would squint, then clench her fists, moving her arms up and down, then squinting until she burst into rage, screaming incoherently and swinging her fists as she approached the author.

To digress for a moment, let's consider the result of this intervention. Martha at certain moments changed some aspects of how she was representing her world in some way that made it possible for her to commit acts of violence. While she was screaming and approaching us, we noticed that her input channel remained visual and her representational system remained kinesthetic. Furthermore, the nominalizations had dropped out of her speech, and color filled her cheeks as she began, for the first time in our experience of her, to breathe deeply. Cause-Effect semantic ill-formedness was still present, but she was no longer placating. Rather, she was blaming furiously and her major output channel was kinesthetic.

M	Input	Representational	Output	Satir	Semantic Ill-	Meta-Model
A	Channel	System	Channel	Category	Formedness	Violation
R						
T	Visual	Kino	Kino	Blaming	De-Nom	Cause-Effect
H						
A	V	K	K	2	Nom.	C.E.

The result of this process of representation was violence. Let us consider how this works: Visual information for Martha was usually taken in and represented as body feelings which in a nominalization were non-movement. (Nominalization is the process by which a verb of natural language is turned into an event or thing, "thingified.") The nominalization of a kinesthetic representation is movement which is frozen into body posture. Thus, when Martha's polarity was played by one of the authors, she saw-felt her own polarity. This served to denominalize her in the following way: A direct biofeedback loop — she felt what she was doing with her own body as the therapist was, at this point, presenting a mirror image, so when she saw-felt him, she felt what was going on in her own body also. Furthermore, the therapist played her dominant polarity more congruently so she responded by communicating the paramessages associated with the less forcefully expressed polarity — blaming. The result was a de-nominalization kinesthetically — blaming communicated kinesthetically, better known as outright violence. Consider now for a moment, if you will, a woman like Martha who rigidly see-feels — she scolds her son in a grating voice of which she is, for the most part, unaware. He, being a child, hear-feels and placates which she see-feels just as one of the authors did. She then responds by denominalizing and exploding into kinesthetic blaming; she hits her son, who becomes more placative upon being attacked by an adult. This only exaggerates Martha's see-feel circuit into an escalating sequence for which she has no controlling resources.

At the risk of seeming too clinical about Martha, we would like to diverge even further from her story for a moment, in order to prepare you to understand what follows. There are two points we wish you to understand before we continue. *First is the theory of pattern disruption.* We have found it most useful in our work to assist our clients in breaking escalating patterns, especially patterns of kinesthetic expression of anger. Many psychotherapists recognize the danger of this type of unchecked escalation and have clients drugged or strapped down to break the mounting pattern of violence. We find this response quite unsatisfactory; drugs and straps do not break the pattern of see-feeling or hear-feeling in a way that will leave the client new choices about how to represent her world and to communicate in the future, nor do drugs and straps make any attempt to integrate both of the valuable parts of human beings. They serve only to suppress the polarity in the same way Martha had been doing all of her life. As see-feeling continues, she will, at some time in the future, explode and the cycle will continue. Nor does drugging and incarceration respect the amazing abilities of human beings to learn new ways of coping and of representing their world. But, most of all, approaches of this nature do not make use of all of the dynamic life that is being represented in an explosion of this nature in a way that will utilize it and make it a source of an integrative experience. We do not intent to harshly scold therapists who use such techniques. We realize that every therapist does the best he can to help people with the tools and skills he has available. We understand that psychotherapy is a very young field and that all of us have much to learn about the vast potential of human beings to learn and to grow, to reorganize the processes by which they represent and communicate their experience. We have much to learn about the ability people have to change in new ways, given the appropriate resources. We are certain that some psychotherapists who have recognized this dilemma have played the polarity of traditional psychotherapy and let their client explode into exhaustion in the belief that the feelings which were being expressed by anger could be discharged permanently. Unfortunately, this does not, in our experience, break the see-feel, hear-feel circuits, nor does this type of activity serve to integrate or re-educate clients in new ways of representing or communicating their experience. Although it may have more value for the client than drugs whose effects are unknown, the basic pattern is unchanged. So, what other choices are available to therapists in these situations?

We suggest that therapists try another alternative — to interrupt the explosion of anger in a way which will enable the client to use the dynamic life force being discharged and, thereby, to integrate the paramessages being expressed, using this energy to break the see-feel—hear-feel circuit in a way that offers clients new choices which are lasting and which enable them to organize their experience differently. This, of course, is easier to say than to do, although it is not as difficult as it, at first, may seem. Consider the problem in the following steps:

First, the case being discussed is that of a see-feeler; her explosion is one which resulted by the therapist's playing polarities. If a therapist wishes to interrupt this escalating pattern, he may do a number of things. He may play the reverse polarity. This will demand all of the congruity the therapist has to present himself as more blaming than the client. The therapist can also require that the client close her eyes, thereby shutting off the see-feel circuit. The problem with this maneuver is that the client may make a visual image in her head which then gets translated into a kinesthetic representation. This may be overcome by a constant demand by the therapist on the client to breathe. He may, in some congruent fashion, demand that she switch representational systems, and shift all that she feels into a pictorial representation. In the following visual representation, we show what has occurred as the therapist played polarity.

Input Channel	Representational System	Output Channel	Satir Category	Semantic Ill-Formedness	Meta-Model Violation	Result
		POLARITY ONE				
V	K	K	1	Cause-Effect	Nom	Incongruent Unstable System
↑		POLARITY TWO			↑	
V	K	K	2	Cause-Effect	φ	Congruent Violence

If you check the two representations above, you will notice that not only are both of these choices and maps of the world rather unsatisfactory for representing Martha's experience, but they are, furthermore, not well sorted and separated polarities according to the criteria of Part II of this book. In order for Martha to begin the process of integration, she must have more choices about how she represents her experience. At this point, she has no choices other than to represent her experience of the world as feelings. Therapeutic goal number one here should be to create an experience which will allow Martha to utilize another of her representational systems. Goal number two should be to have that representational system feed into an output channel which is safe for her to use to denominalize herself.

As Martha came screaming and swinging her fists, both authors, simultaneously, firmly and congruently interrupted this explosion as it reached a peak of frenzy by demanding in a blaming way that she stop and close her eyes, and allow all that she felt to evolve itself into a picture in her mind's eye. She paused, as if startled; the demand was made even stronger and more congruently. Her eyes closed and she began to squint.

Therapist: What do you see now?

Martha: (Yelling) Nothing (her voice beginning to trail off). God damn it. . . .

Therapist: Look harder till you *see!*

Martha: I can't. I can't (whining, but her fists still closed).

Therapist: (The therapist told her to breathe deeply and she did so to let the tension in her body come out as a picture. His voice changing to softness, he continued to coax her until her facial expression changed slightly.) Now, what do you *see?*

Martha: Yes, I can't tell what it is . . . it's foggy. . . .

Therapist: Take a breath, let the image become clear, look closer, let it come.

Martha: (Beginning to sob) Shit . . . oh, shit. (She begins to clench her fists as if to return to a frenzy.)

Therapist: No, don't interfere this time, just let it come and look. You have been running for too long and you have had too much pain, so this time bear it for awhile and you will learn (softly).

Martha: (Crying now) My baby, my baby, he . . . (sobbing).

Therapist: Tell me what you *see,* describe your *image* as *clearly* as you can.

Martha: He looks so scared, and so hurt . . . (breaking into tears, but beginning to clench her fists).

Therapist: No, just *look,* and *see,* and *describe* just this once. You have carried this for too, too long. Just *see* what you *see,* and *describe* it to me.

Martha began at this point to describe her son as frightened and hurt. She sobbed and sobbed.

This is only the beginning, and too often, in our experience, therapists stop at a point such as this and let all of these energies be exhausted. Again we moved to help Martha more. Martha now has reversed her process — she is taking kinesthetic representations and making visual representations for them. The see-feel cycle is at least temporarily interrupted.

Input Channel	Representational System	Output Channel	Satir Categroy
K————V————Auditory — ϕ ——1—— ————M.R.			

Martha had begun the process of change. We then proceeded to try to sort the appropriate input channels into the associated representational system. During this time, we had Martha watch the image of her baby and placed her body in the position from which she had previously placated, asking her to watch the image closely as we moved her body. The image changed; she was frightened at first and we reassured her. She described seeing herself; she said she looked mean and angry in her picture. She described herself as having a fierce-looking face and intense eyes.

> *Therapist:* As you look at this part of yourself, watch her closely, and tell her how you feel as you see her; be sure to keep a clear picture, and watch her expression as you tell her this.

This request has the presupposition that the client will express her kinesthetic sensation verbally while at the same time maintaining a visual representation.

> *Martha:* Please don't make me . . .
> *Therapist:* (Interrupting) Tell her what you feel as you see her in your mind's eye.
> *Martha:* I feel afraid.
> *Therapist:* Tell her how, specifically.
> *Martha:* You . . .
> *Therapist:* Tell her how you feel afraid in your body.
> *Martha:* I feel tense in my back and shaky in my stomach. I'm afraid of you . . . of what you make me do.
> *Therapist:* Watch her face! What do you see? . . . How does she look?
> *Martha:* She looks disgusted.
> *Therapist:* How, specifically?
> *Martha:* She is scowling, and shaking her head back and forth. (Martha is shaking her head no.)
> *Therapist:* Describe what you see — do not do it. (The therapist stops Martha from moving her head.) Is she still shaking her head?
> *Martha:* Yes.
> *Therapist:* As you watch and listen to her, what does she say?

Martha: I don't hear anyth . . . .

Therapist: Listen more closely. There, do you hear? What does she say as you watch her lips and her mouth move?

Martha: Twisting her head as if to hear, she smiles a little smirk.

Therapist: What did she say to you?

Martha: (Chuckling) She said I'm a dumb bell, and to stop whining, and to defend myself.

Therapist: How is that funny?

Martha: Well, it's me but the words are the same things my mother always told me (her chuckling turns to a soft sobbing). I swore I'd never be like her. Damn it, damn it (still soft and mumbling).

Therapist: Now, Martha, watch her closely, and tell how you're not like her. Watch her closely, and listen as you do this. Say *Martha*.

Martha: Martha, I'm not like you. I . . . I . . . I'm — mmmm — nice to people, and kind of soft, warm to them — I don't hurt them.

Therapist: What does she say as you watch her? Listen closely.

Martha: . . . She, she says I'm too weak, too easily pushed around.

Therapist: How does she look as she says this to you?

Martha: She doesn't look mad now; she looks concerned, sort of worried about me.

Therapist: Tell her about your worries for her, and watch and listen.

Martha: You a . . . a . . . I . . . I am worried about you. You hurt people by coming out so suddenly and so meanly . . . then you end up being lonely. Even I fight to keep you away.

Therapist: Now, listen ever so carefully, and watch her, as you listen.

Martha: (Smiling, with concerned expression) She looks . . . sort of brave, if you know what I mean. She says she can take . . . take it.

Therapist: How do you feel about her now, as you look at her?

Martha: Well, it's the first time I ever . . . well . . . kind of liked her at all, you know.

Therapist: Martha, watch her, and as you do, ask her what, specifically, she wants.

Martha: (Interrupting) What *do* you want? She wants me to let her help me stand up so . . . well . . . so she doesn't need to burst out. She wants me to see that I don't always need to be so wishy-washy.

Therapist: Would you like that? (Martha nods yes.) Tell her.

Martha: I feel I need you, not all at one time though but I do need to be braver and stronger. I do.

Therapist: Tell her what you want for yourself; watch her and tell her what you want for yourself.

Martha: I want your . . . well . . . good things, but I also want to be soft and not hurt anybody . . . physically and not lose total control, you know . . .

Therapist: What's her reply? Listen — watch her.

Martha: She agrees we could do it. She's smiling and . . .

Therapist: Martha, as you see her smiling, strong and brave, and not needing to take control over you, knowing that you can have both her toughness and your own tenderness when either is appropriate, let your hands come up slowly, grasping the picture before you, ever so slowly, watching her face. (Martha's eyes are still closed. She raises her hands and grasps the air a foot in front of her.) Now, slowly seeing her and feeling yourself pull her closer to you slowly . . . so slowly . . . until you feel her enter and become part of yourself, seeing what you see and feeling what you feel. That's right. (Martha pulls her hands slowly until they touch her chest. As she did, she took a deep breath, and then another, relaxing her body and smiling.) What do you feel as you let this become part of you?

Martha: (Smiling) It's kind of weird . . .

Therapist: What is?

Martha: I feel a tingling in my chest . . . feel good . . . but . . .

Therapist: Just let this spread and spread and fill your whole body. As it does so, what do you see?

Martha: Bobby (her son). I miss him . . .

Therapist: How do you feel?

Martha: Still tingling, but it is all over my body now.

Therapist: Now, Martha, let your eyes open, slowly feeling your body, and seeing what you see as you feel yourself . . . slowly, that's it . . . tell what you see.

Martha: I see people — they look bright. . . . I mean the colors are so bright and I see you (speaking to one of the authors).

Therapist: And how do you feel as you look at me?

Martha: Still tingling. It feels good. I'm so relaxed but yet so — so, well, awake, kind of. I feel good.

Therapist: Martha, too often therapy looks good but is not effective. May we test you?

Martha: What? No, I heard you. How?

Therapist: That spoils it; will you trust me?

Martha: Yes (tilting her head in confusion, but still glowing and smiling and breathing deeply).

Therapist: (The therapist began at this point to play the same polarity that elicited such a violent response, placating Martha and asking her to please [in a grating voice] not be so hard on herself.)

Martha: Martha laughed uproariously and, forcing a grin, looked at the therapist and jokingly said, "You're disgusting; you need help."

Although neither of the therapists has seen Martha again and there are still many parts of her which could use therapeutic assistance, this is an example of the power humans have to change. She called us twice on the phone; once, two months later to tell us she was alive and well in the Midwest. She was happy and endeavoring to begin a new life. A second call came six months later from a joyous Martha who had with her once again her son; she expressed gratitude for the two hours we gave her and promised to buy a copy of this book. We are not suggesting that one therapeutic session is ever all that a client needs, but, rather, that a great deal can happen in a short time when we, as therapists, respect our client's ability to grow and change when given the resources to do so. Most important, we wish you to realize the necessity of giving clients choices about how they represent the world, especially when they have rigid fuzzy-function patterns.

Let us return now to Martha and see what can be learned from this session. In the last change that we discussed, Martha was representing the world by the following process:

Input Channel	Representational System	Output Channel	Satir Category	Semantic Ill-Formedness	Meta-Model Violation
K	V	A	1	M.R.	ϕ

As the therapist placed Martha's body in a placating posture she had previously used, the only possibility for change was the content of her visual representation — she became herself instead of her son.

Input Channel	Representational System	Output Channel	Satir Stance	Semantic Ill-Formedness	Meta-Model Violation
K	V	A	1	M.R.	ø

The above is a process of representation which is safe to denominalize. The therapist then assists the client to denominalizing, putting movements, action, and process into the visual representation, at the same time working to simultaneously build a kinesthetic representational system, sorting Martha's incongruency until she had two congruent models of the world.

	Input Channel	Representational System	Output Channel	Satir Stance	Semantic Ill-Formedness	Meta-Model Violation
1.	K	K	A external	1	M.R.	Del
2.	A	V	A internal	2	C.E.	Del

These polarities were then integrated in both the visual and kinesthetic representational systems simultaneously, the results being:

Input Channel	Representational System	Output Channel	Satir Stance	Semantic Ill-Formedness	Meta-Model Violation
K	K	K			
V	V	V			

Although many aspects of Martha's life will still contain ill-formed representations, she has a new reference structure of see-seeing and feel-feeling at the same time. This will greatly affect her ability to cope every time she chooses to use this new learning. What more can be expected from a few hours and a chance meeting?

The preceding case of Martha is not an exceptional one in our work. We have found fuzzy functions to be the process behind many painful and inadequate coping systems in our clients. Cases of sadism, for example, have been identified as see-feel circuits in which visual input of another's pain was represented as kinesthetic pleasure. We have had clients whose asthma was the result of see-feel, hear-feel representation of other's aggression toward them stored in their own bodies (especially their neck and throat). The value of working with fuzzy functions is that we are able to give our clients choices about where and when they use these fuzzy functions directly — this has great potential for therapy in and by itself. There is, however, even more to be gained from an understanding of these processes. Very often in therapy, just when something begins to happen, a client will seem to lose the ability to hear or see, or both. He might become agitated in some way which interrupts his progress and growth and the development of new choices. We have found in our own work that very often we can reverse these interruptions simply by paying attention to the shifts which our clients make in their body postures. Fuzzy functions, we have found, are associated with distinctive body postures. These postures may be different for each person with whom we work, but are, in each case, quite noticeable. In times of stress, some clients lift their chin up, others push their chin out in front of them, others scrunch their shoulders together, and some squint their eyes. These are typical. They all share similar outcomes — they all serve to identify a fuzzy function. We have found that rearranging our clients' postures back to a more relaxed one and then asking them to breathe very often is all that is needed to continue a therapeutic session on a course which is accomplishing something. Sometimes a maneuver such as this will set off powerful reactions. If a client is see-feeling a strong emotion and tries to cut that emotion off by lifting and stiffening his neck, and we move his neck back, he will come into contact with feelings which have been the source of great coping difficulties.

Some rather interesting research has been done in this area. Gerald Schuchman and Ernest J. Burgi in 1971 reported that jaw position has a profound effect on hearing. By shifting the position of the jaw bone, differences in sensitivity to pure tone could be increased. Also, sensitivity for threshold sensitivity increased on the average of 15db. What this means to the psychotherapist is simply that, by shifting a client's jaw position, you will increase his ability to hear. Also, by paying close attention to our clients' jaw position, we can learn when they are hearing and when they are not.

Altshuler and Comalli have reported findings in the area of body tilt and ability to localize sound. Many studies of this nature have been done. What we as therapists can learn is not just to read these journals but also to pay attention to our own experience in a new way. Try a little exercise, if you will:

Have someone speak to you about anything. As they do so in a fashion that does not require you to reply, try shifting your own jaw bone to different positions and listen to the effect on your own ability to hear. We have all had the experience of fading out of a conversation, but have you ever paid attention to any posture changes you use to accomplish this? This will be an opportunity to learn, not only about yourself, but about how your clients also use posture to affect their hearing. Next, try all kinds of combinations of moving your head from left to right and tilting your body, pulling your shoulders together, and any other combination that comes to mind. You might try a posture of one of your clients who does seem to hear you too well and see if changing to his posture affects your own hearing.

The changes you notice in your own ability to hear will be exaggerated in your clients in times of stress or when discussing emotionally charged issues. Helping them to keep breathing and maintaining a posture which allows them to hear will be a big asset. Virginia Satir said to a client one time, "It is easy to feel down when you keep looking down." We suggest that you try it for an hour and experience the truth of her words. There are many body tuning techniques which we use in our work. These will be detailed more precisely in a later volume. Most of these you can find by exploration if you are willing to simply explore with yourself. People who squint complain of great difficulty in seeing, or often state:

I can't see what you're saying to them.

People who have great difficulty with visual imagery can be assisted in learning these techniques by paying close attention to eye-scanning patterns — as a cursory review of recent Rapid Eye Movement (REM) research will show.

Body tuning can be an amazing asset in therapy when used to assist clients in using their senses to the utmost potential while dealing with stressful portions of their model of the world. We intend to do much more work in this area in the coming year. For now, we would like to mention this briefly so those of you who wish to explore this area will have the opportunity.

SUMMARY OF PART III

Fuzzy functions are the processes for representing the world which are the basis of semantic ill-formedness, when our clients do not have choices about what they see-feel or hear-feel, feel-hear, etc. Since semantic ill-formedness is the source of much of the pain we see and hear in therapy, we would like briefly to review the possibilities of fuzzy functions and their outcomes.

Input		Representation	Type of Semantic Ill-Formedness
Visual	to	Kinesthetic	= Cause-effect / You make me sad
V———————►K			= C.E.
Auditory	to	Kinesthetic	= Cause-effect / You make me sad
A———————►K			= C.E.

Input		Representation	Type of Semantic Ill-Formedness
Kinesthetic	to	Visual	= Mind reading / I can see when he's scared.
K———————►V			= MR
Kinesthetic	to	Auditory	= MR / I know what he's thinking.
K———————► A			= MR
Visual	to	Auditory	= MR
V———————► A			= MR
Auditory	to	Visual	= MR
A———————►V			= MR
All the Mind-reading functions			= Lost Performative / He knows it's wrong. She's crazy not to see it.

FOOTNOTES FOR PART III

1. In Volume I of *Magic*, we identified three types of semantic ill-formedness:

Cause-Effect   Mind-Reading   Lost Performative

This third type, Lost Performative, is exemplified by utterances such as:

All smokers are crazy.
It is true that money implies happiness.
Good girls don't hit boys.

Lost Performative is the case in which the speaker assumes that his model of the world is the world or, minimally, assumes that his model of the world should be everyone's model. This is essentially a violation of the map-territory distinction. As mentioned in the analysis in *Magic I*, this phenomenon is a special case of deletion — in which the performative which carries the map-territory distinction has been deleted. We would also mention that, if the reader finds it more satisfying, it is possible to consider the Lost Performative semantic ill-formedness a special case of Mind Reading, in which the speaker generalizes his model of the world, not only to the person to whom he is speaking, as in:

You must be bored, listening to me describe my problems.

but to the entire world as in:

It's boring to listen to people describe their problems.

2.   Here we are listing and discussing only the two most common fuzzy functions which are initiated by stimuli external to the person experiencing the phenomenon. We have, however, encountered the other logical possibilities, namely:

(a) When the client takes information arriving in the visual channel and represents it auditorially. For example, the client is watching a second person who waves his hand in a gesture which is similar to a gesture which commonly means *go away*, while simultaneously uttering some noise, not words. The client in this case subsequently claimed that she heard the man yell the words, *Go away!* This is an example of the fuzzy function see-hear.

(b) When the client takes information arriving in the auditory channel and represents it visually. For example, the client hears a second person who yells the words, *get out of my way*, at the same time that he throws his jacket down on the chair between them. The client in this case later claimed that he had thrown his jacket at her. This is an example of the fuzzy function hear-see.

3.   Again, here we are listing and discussing only the two most common fuzzy functions associated with the semantic ill-formedness Mind Reading. We have also encountered the other logical possibilities, namely:

(a) When the client takes information which is stored visually and distorts his auditory input to match the visually stored material — for example, people who have an *image* of themselves as worthless will tend to *hear* complementary remarks from others as sarcastic or ironic; thus, see-hearing.

(b) When the client takes information which is stored auditorially and distorts his visual input to make it match. For example, someone whom the client knows has consistently been sarcastic toward her in the past. They are both standing in a group and the client is speaking, describing a recent experience. As she tells a portion of her experience which is amusing — indeed, some of the people in the group laugh — she notices that this other person is smiling. She will interpret this information received visually to be consistent with her auditorially stored information — in this case, that he is smiling sarcastically at her present behavior, not that he is enjoying the story which she is telling; thus, hear-seeing.

PART IV

Family Therapy – The Delicate Flower

If you did nothing more when you have a family together than to make it possible for them to really look at each other, really touch each other, and listen to each other, you would have already swung the pendulum in the direction of a new start.

> Virginia Satir, p. 61 of Chapter IV, Intervention for Congruence, in *Helping Families to Change*. Edited by Tiffany, et al. The High Plains Comprehensive Community Mental Health Center, Hays, Kansas.

A flower is a marvelous piece of life; although we can plant a seed and assist the growth process, we humans as yet cannot create a live flower. We can crossbreed, transplant, cultivate, and graft flowers, but we cannot create one from scratch unless it has no life in it, unless it is made only of paper or plastic. Another characteristic of flowers and plants is that they grow best in their native environment, and, although they will grow in another environment, it takes much more support from those cultivating their growth for a flower to have the same heartiness and chance of reaching its full potential. But sometimes, even in a flower's native environment, although it may exist for its full life cycle, it is scraggly and bears few blooms. Sometimes these wild flowers even become so constricted that they choke each other and become sick and die. Flowers achieve their greatest growth and fullest beauty and bear the sweetest fruit when they are nurtured with appropriate resources in their native habitat and given adequate room to grow. We believe this process we described for flowers is also true for people in many ways. The following chapter on family therapy represents this belief. Family therapy is probably the most difficult form of therapy in which to become proficient, but it is also probably the most rewarding and enriching approach to therapy if it is performed with loving skill.

OVERALL STRATEGY FOR ASSISTING FAMILIES TO CHANGE

The techniques which are essential for family therapy are not, in themselves, different from those of individual therapy. They are, however, organized in a different fashion. This means that, while Meta-model questions, representational systems, and polarities remain the key principles, they are organized and used in a different way. These principles are reorganized around the concept of a family as a system. To accept the family as the system unit for therapy is to use an overall strategy to work with the family as if it were one living organism, each member being an essential part and resource and, therefore, crucial to the satisfactory behavior of the organism as a whole. Consequently, behavior of all the parts or members of the family organism will affect all the members in the same way — conflicting or not conflicting parts of one human being's model of the world will have an effect on his behavior and ability to cope. What all this implies for family therapy is that, in the same way that conflicting paramessages produce incongruity, stifling inability to cope, and painful hopelessness in one human being, so, too, conflicting models of the world in the family organism held can produce chaos, paralyzing rules, and, thus, prevent family members from being connected with each other in a way which is nourishing to all of the members of the family.

What, then, are the specific differences between family and individual therapy? Therapy for an individual has been described, basically, in the two volumes of *Magic* as a process using the Meta-model distinctions, representational systems, incongruity questions with a client to identify the portion of his model of the world which is impoverished in some way which prevents him from coping, having choices, and getting what he wants from life. Once this is done, the client's behavior will make sense, given the premises from which he has constructed his representations. The therapist then has many choices about how to proceed. In *Magic I* we said that no person is bad, sick or crazy, no matter how bizarre his behavior might at first appear. Similarly, in family therapy we see no member as the cause of the problems in coping, nor do we label any member or any part of any member as bad, sick or crazy. We begin with the premise that the system (family organism as a whole) has some portion of its shared model of the world impoverished in a way that prevents the processes going on in that system from being nourishing.

One of the most dramatic ways in which therapy will differ in these two contexts is that the patterns of behavior which at first appear quite bizarre to the therapist in the context of individual therapy will make much more sense when that individual is seen and heard in the context of family therapy. The family, itself, is one of the most important contexts to which the individual must adapt himself, and, thus, the patterns which strike the therapist as peculiar when seen and heard without the other family members being present will be more understandable in the context of the family's patterns. In other words, the therapist has immediately available before him the individual's most important context — the one which more than any other context has contributed to his generalizations about life — his model of the world. This, of course, has a profound effect on the therapist's choice of therapeutic techniques. Take the technique of enactment, for example. One of the values of an enactment technique is that it allows the therapist to see and to hear for himself the way in which the client models his experience. By having the client re-live an experience from the past and then comparing the *client's* ability to make sense out of it with the *therapist's* ability to make sense out of it, the therapist has an excellent example of the kind of modeling processes which the client typically employs in constructing his model of his experience. By using an enactment technique in individual therapy, the therapist has the opportunity to identify the specific ways in which the client uses the three universals of human modeling to cope or to fail to cope. The therapist using this technique might, for example, discover that the client systematically fails to hear what the other people in the enactment are presenting auditorially — what they are saying to him. In the context of family therapy, however, there is no need for the therapist to rely on a re-creation of some scene from the past as the communication process unfolding before him is the real thing — the process which forms the basis for the client's modeling. By carefully attending to the communication process — the presence or absence of incongruity in the communications among family members, or the systematic avoidance or deletion of certain types of messages — and by questioning the family members about what they are most aware of, the therapist can identify the deletions, distortions, and generalizations which are preventing the family members from achieving together the experiences which they want.

The second way in which family therapy is dramatically different from individual therapy is that, in individual therapy, the individual, no matter how incongruent or split he may be, no matter how many parts he may be expressing, no matter how conflicting these different parts are, occupies the same body. In family therapy, a number of individuals who occupy different bodies are involved; consequently, there is the possibility that the therapist's interventions may change the family system in some way which will lead to the family members' deciding to dissolve the family as an organism. For the remainder of this discussion, we make the assumption that the breaking up of a family is the least acceptable outcome for the family therapist. There is no parallel in individual therapy.

The assumption that the breaking up of the family is the least acceptable outcome in family therapy places certain constraints on the therapist. First of all, we recommend that the therapist determine as one of the very first items of business with the family exactly what goal they have for themselves. This will allow the therapist to decide whether he is willing to attempt to work with the family toward those goals within the constraints of family therapy. The therapist may, for example, decide that he is unwilling to accept the constraints of family therapy but offer to work with individual members in individual therapy.[1]

Now, given the assumption that the breaking up of the family system is the least acceptable outcome, how, specifically, does the therapist behave differently in the context of family therapy when compared to individual therapy? In our experience, in every family or couple we have encountered, we have identified the particular form of semantic ill-formedness called Cause-Effect semantic ill-formedness — the situation in which one member of the family is represented as causing another family member to experience some feeling or emotion. For example, statements such as:

> ... *My husband makes me feel wonderful whenever he looks at me that way.*

or

> ... *She disappoints me greatly when she doesn't listen to me.*

In each case, the speaker of these sentences is accepting a representation of his experience in which his feelings are determined or caused by the actions of another. The linguistic representation of Cause-Effect semantic ill-formedness translates, when mapped into the world of the speaker's experience, into specific hear-feel and see-feel circuits — the subject of Part III of this volume. Thus, one of the most common ways in which people maintain couple and family relationships is in maintaining a set of positive highly valued fuzzy functions. Since the constraint in family therapy is to maintain the family as an organism, for the therapist to challenge the Cause-Effect semantic ill-formedness or the fuzzy functions which are its basis is to attack the very foundations of the family system. This is the major way in which family and individual therapy differ. In indivudal therapy, there is a positive value in challenging any and all expressions of Cause-Effect semantic ill-formedness, while, in family therapy, the therapist must make conscious decisions about the outcome of challenging Cause-Effect semantic ill-formedness in terms of maintaining the family structure. The sensitivity which the therapist shows in selecting the particular Cause-Effect relations with which he will deal explicitly is much of the art of fast, effective family therapy. Later in this part of the book we will present general guidelines for the way the therapist can make effective decisions about which forms of Cause-Effect semantic ill-formedness he may usefully challenge.

Within the differences peculiar to family therapy, the therapist employs a familiar three-step process to assist the family in the process of change and growth: (1) Identification of both what the family wants for itself as a unit and what its present resources are; (2) The evolving of the family system from its present state to the desired state; and (3) The integration of the new choices and patterns of interaction created by the family and therapist in the work sessions. These three steps parallel the three steps in incongruity work called Identifying Incongruities, Sorting Incongruities into Polarities, and Integrating Incongruities. As we more fully develop the principles of family therapy, the parallels will become even more obvious.

IDENTIFICATION OF PRESENT STATE AND DESIRED STATE FOR THE FAMILY

As in any form of therapy, the therapist, himself, serves as a model for communication. In beginning therapy with a family, we have found it particularly useful to be very direct about what the goals of the therapy will be. Specifically, we have found it useful to ask each of the family members directly to state what he wants from the therapeutic session. This may be accomplished by asking any of the following questions:

> What are your hopes for yourself and your family in therapy?
>
> How, specifically, would you like you and your family to change?
>
> What do you want for yourself and your family?
>
> If you could change yourself and your family in any way you want, what changes would you make?
>
> How would you and your family be different if you all changed in the very best of ways from this experience?

The answer which the therapist receives to such questions will, of course, be in the form of a Surface Structure of English — a Surface Structure which is subject to all the well-formed-in-therapy conditions. In addition, as each of the family members reply, he will unconsciously select predicates which will reveal to the attentive therapist what his representational systems are. The Meta-model distinctions apply here and provide the therapist with a way of effectively beginning the process of communicating clearly with each of the family members while simultaneously clarifying both for himself and the family members the agreed-upon goals of the therapeutic work. The outcome of this process is some mutually agreed upon set of therapuetic goals. This identifies the state of living which the family wishes to achieve for itself.

At the same time that the therapist is working with the family to clarify the therapeutic goals, he is watching and listening to the various family members express themselves: their hopes, fears, and needs as they perceive them. We have found it very useful as a natural and integral part of the process to ask different family members to report their experiences of this ongoing process. By requesting this behavior and attending closely to the response of the family members, we learn a great deal about the modeling principles which they use to construct the model for their experience. We quote several brief excerpts from beginning family therapy sessions by way of example:

> *Therapist:* And you, Betty, as the wife and mother in this family, what are your hopes for yourself and your family? What changes would you like to make?
>
> *Betty:* Well, I see so much resentment and bitterness in the family ... I never have a chance to relax; just look at my husband, sitting there ignoring me just like he always does.
>
> *Therapist:* How do you know that Jim, your husband, is ignoring you, Betty?
>
> *Betty:* What do you mean, "How do I know he's ignoring me?" — anyone can clearly see that he is. .... He hasn't looked at me once the whole time I've been talking. I don't even ...

Notice that in these few lines the therapist can already identify a number of important patterns. Betty uses primarily visual predicates *(see, look, see, clearly, looked)*, universal quantifiers *(never, always, anyone, not once, whole time)* and visual input as the basis of mind reading (complex equivalence: *He's ignoring me = He hasn't looked at me once*). Betty's use of both visual predicates and universal quantifiers (syntactic correlate of Satir Category 2 — blaming) fits a common pattern which we discussed in Part II of this volume — specifically, the congruence of a blamer and the use of visual predicates.

> *Therapist:* Hold it, Betty (interrupting). Jim, I'm curious about something. Were you ignoring Betty just now?
>
> *Jim:* No, I heard what she said.
>
> *Therapist:* Tell me, Jim, what was your experience when you heard her say what she said?
>
> *Jim:* Well, she tells me a lot that I'm not much good, so I'm kinda used to it, you know. . . . I just . . .
>
> *Therapist:* Wait a minute, Jim, what did you hear Betty actually say?
>
> *Jim:* Well, I . . . uh, well, I don't exactly remember the words that she used, but she sounded real mad — you know, I've heard her sound that way lots of times before, I get the message . . .

The attentive therapist can extract another pattern from the few additional lines. Note that Jim uses a large number of auditory predicates *(heard, said, tells, words, sounded, sound)* yet he is unable to recall the words — apparently, he is responding to the tonality of Betty's communication. Furthermore, his communication verifies that the exchange — Betty's blame — is a pattern which he knows well. Notice that he also uses complex equivalence *(She sounded real mad = She tells me that I'm not much good)* as the basis for mind reading. One of the recurrent patterns which distinguishes families which are relatively open to change and growth from those which are relatively closed is the degree to which the family members use feedback as opposed to calibration (see Bateson, p. 9 in Jackson, Vol. 2) in their communication with one another. In other words, if each time Jim hears an angry tone of voice from Betty, he "knows" that she is telling him that he is not much good, or if each time that Betty sees Jim not looking at her when she is speaking she "knows" that he is ignoring her, each of these family members is relatively calibrated to each other's communications — they have no well-developed channels for getting or asking for feedback. That is, rather than asking Jim whether he is paying attention and whether he wants to respond to her (asking for feedback), Betty makes the mind-reading assumption that, since he is not looking at her, he is ignoring her. Typically, even after Jim states that he was paying attention to her, Betty will deny it — she is calibrated on the partial analogue communication from Jim — whether he is looking at her, a calibration that not even his further claim will affect. Betty and Jim have a set of habits which constitute calibrated communication and thus allows little room for change.

> *Joan:* I want to answer but feel afraid, I . . .
> *Therapist:* Afraid of what?
> *Joan:* Well, I . . . I don't know whether I ought to talk about
> this . . . Mom always . . .
> *Joyce:* (Interrupting) Of course, dear; please express yourself
> freely (spoken with a harsh, shrill voice, left arm extended
> with finger pointing at her daughter, Joan).
> *Joan:* I think I'll just wait . . . I don't feel comfortable right
> now.
> *Therapist:* Max (turning to the father), what did you experi-
> ence just now during the exchange between your daughter
> and your wife?
> *Max:* Yeah, well, I just don't understand what you want from
> us, Joan; you start to say something, your mother encour-
> ages you and then you stop — you always frustrate us that
> way.

Here, in this exchange, the therapist, by asking the father/husband to present his experience of the communication between his wife and his daughter, learns that for him (Max) the communication which his wife presented (analogue blaming with verbally incongruent message) to his daughter is represented only by the verbal portion. In fact, he blames Joan, the daughter *(you always frustrate us that way)*, for responding to the analogue portions of the messages with which her mother presented her. The use of the plural pronouns *(us, us)* shows the therapist the way the father perceives and represents the alignment of people in the family system.

These types of examples could be numerous — the point, however, is simply that, during this initial stage of family therapy, the therapist is acting to both come to understand the state that the family wants to achieve and the state in which they presently are living. The larger patterns of communication among family members can be usefully organized along the following dimensions:

a. The representational system of each family member;
b. The Satir category of each family member;
c. The recurrent patterns of communication incongruity of each family member;
d. The primary input channel for getting information for each family member;

e. The primary output channels for expressing themselves for each family member;

f. The kind and extent of semantic ill-formedness for each family member.

As we have discussed in detail in the previous sections, these pieces of information will yield enough information to allow the therapist a coherent understanding of the present state of each of the family members. We turn now to the way in which these patterns fit together to make up the family system.

Basic to any discussion of the description of the family as a system is an understanding of the process by which people first come together to form couples and families. We call this the Pairing Principle.

THE PAIRING PRINCIPLE

What we have noticed time and time again is that the distribution of representational systems and Satir categories in family systems and in polarities is the same. Specifically, in Part II of this volume, we pointed out that the most frequent and effective incongruity-into-polarity sorting was a sorting which resulted in two polarities: one, a visual/Satir category 2 and the other, a kinesthetic/Satir category 1. Parallelly, in the context of couples and family systems work, the most frequent distribution of representational systems and Satir categories is one in which one of the parenting family members is a visual/Satir category 2 and the other, a kinesthetic/Satir category 1. For the moment, we restrict ourselves to a discussion of the minimum family system — the couple. This particular pattern of distribution of representational systems and Satir categories makes sense to us. Specifically, consider the Meta-tactic for incongruity work of playing polarity. A therapist wishes to elicit the weaker of two polarities to assist the client in fully expressing that polarity as a step on the way to integration. We designate the two polarities by the symbols P_1 and P_2. Suppose, now, that the polarity symbolized by P_1 is the stronger of the two polarities. In order to elicit the weaker of the two polarities, P_2, the therapist plays, not the weaker one, but P_1, the stronger of the two — the one that the client is presently displaying. When the therapist plays P_1 more forcefully than the client, the result is that the client flips polarities, playing P_2. In fact, as we mentioned in that section, if the therapist fails to observe polarity principle and attempts to convince the client, offer advice, in such a way that the client perceives the therapist as playing the weaker polarity, the client is locked into playing the opposite polarity, and, typically, never takes responsibility for the other polarity, never expresses it fully and is, therefore, unable to integrate it.

Consider now the polarity principle in the context of pairing and the formations of stable couple relations. Off goes some hypothetical male; let's call him Sam. Sam has the standard, frequently occurring incongruity of having two models of the world which conflict in some areas of his behavior but not so much that he is immobilized — one of these models is kinesthetic and placating (Satir 1) — call it S_1 — and the other is visual and blaming (Satir 2) — call it S_2. Sam's most highly developed polarity is S_1. One day, Sam runs into (being a kinesthetic) a woman named Louise. Louise also has the most frequent polarity split — one polarity, the stronger, is visual and blaming — call it L_1 — while her other polarity is kinesthetic and placating, call it L_2. When these two well-meaning people come into contact, we have the following situation:

Louise	Sam
L_1 (visual/blaming)	S_1 (kinesthetic/placating)
L_2 (kinesthetic/placating)	S_2 (visual/blaming)

Specifically, when these two people make contact, they perceive one another's most dominant polarity as follows:

Louise	Sam
L_1 (visual/blaming)	S_1 (kinesthetic/placating)

By the polarity principle, we can predict the outcome of this encounter — that is, each of the people is perceived by the other as playing his partner's weaker polarity:

$$L_1 = S_2$$
and
$$L_2 = S_1$$

Translating this visual representation into words, we observe that, since each of the people is playing the other's weaker polarity, we have the situation in which the therapist fails to take the polarity principle into account, inadvertently playing the client's weaker polarity. The client thereby gets stuck in the dominant polarity, fails to fully express his weaker polarity fully and therefore does not integrate. In fact, the client comes to depend upon the therapist to continue to play his weaker polarity.[2] In the context of a couple relationship, the result is a highly stable system — each member of the system depending upon the other to continue to play his less fully expressed polarity. We are not suggesting that the polarity principle is the *only* principle by which individuals come together and form lasting relationships, simply that this principle accounts for much of our experience in couple and family work. Let's carry the hypothetical example a bit further. Suppose, all other things being equal, that Louise and Sam find each other attractive, and they decide to have a traditional family. They have a child; we'll call him Jim. As Jim grows up, he sees and hears his parents and, as with most children, adopts them as models for his own growth. Jim, however, is faced with a problem. His parents conflict in certain ways — they have models for their own behavior which are inconsistent with one another: one being visual and blaming and the other being kinesthetic and placating. Watching and listening to his parents handle stress and cope with life's demands provides Jim with many choices about his own model of the world (albeit, unconsciously) — unfortunately inconsistent with one another. How, then, will young Jim solve this problem? We can hardly expect him to accept the models displayed by both of his parents and integrate them — his parents with the presumed advantages of age and education failed to accomplish this for themselves. The most likely outcome is that Jim will "identify" more strongly with one of his parents than with the other and adopt that parent's model of the world as his dominant or more fully expressed polarity. Of course, Jim, being the loving son that he is, will want to indicate in some way that he also loves and respects his other parent. He may show this, of course, by adopting his other parent's model of the world as a less fully expressed conflicting polarity.

Louise   **Sam**
L_1 (visual and blaming) S_1 (kinesthetic and placating)

Jim
J_1 (kinesthetic and placating)
J_2 (visual and blaming)

Now all we need do is to construct another family with a daughter named Marie, whose parents have the same polarity game going in which Marie selects as follows:

Marie
M_1 (visual and blaming)
M_2 (kinesthetic and placating)

and we have the proper basis for a new cycle of polarity pairing.

There are other possible outcomes to these patterns. For example, if the original couple, Louise and Sam, each have polarities which are relatively balanced — that is, nearly equally well expressed, then they will likely engage in what Satir has called the Yo-Yo game. When Louise, for example, is expressing her polarity L_1 (visual and blaming), Sam expresses his primary S_1 (kinesthetic and placating). Suppose, now, that Louise flips strongly over to her secondary polarity L_2 (kinesthetic and placating). We then have the following situation:

Louise	Sam
L_2 (kinesthetic and placating)	S_2 (kinesthetic and placating)

By the polarity principle, Louise has just performed a maneuver which in the context of therapy is a Meta-tactic — namely, she is playing Sam's polarity. If she is congruent enough in her flip, then it follows, by the polarity principle, that Sam will flip to his secondary polarity, stabilizing the system. We then have:

Louise	Sam
L_2 (kinesthetic and placating)	S_2 (visual and blaming)

In our experience this Yo-Yo pattern will vary from family to family so that a single, complete cycle (in this case, both Louise and Sam return to their primary polarities) can take from 30 seconds, to months, to even years. Satir has termed this type of polarity flip one of the possible movements in a family stress "ballet." People caught in such movements rarely have any consciousness of the regularity of their behavior.

Consider, now, the outcome of this type of experience on young Jim — assuming, of course, that Louise and Sam stabilize the ballet sufficiently to have children. In this case, young Jim's experience is somewhat more bewildering, and the choice he must make to love and respect each of his parents is less clear. One particularly unfortunate choice for young Jim would be to mix his polarities so that he is maximally incongruent at all times.

Louise	Sam

L_1 (visual and blaming) S_1 (kinesthetic and placating)

L_2 (kinesthetic and placating) S_2 (visual and blaming)

Jim

J_1 (visual and placating)

J_2 (kinesthetic and blaming)

Notice, in particular, Jim's minor polarity — J_2 (Kinesthetic and blaming) — the reader will recognize this combination as a portion of the description of Martha, the woman who found herself an uncontrollable child-beater, in the last part of this volume. Furthermore, since Jim is consistently incongruent in his communication, others will respond to him in a similar fashion, and he is likely to find the world a really peculiar experience.

Another frequent response which children make to the task that confronts Jim is to decide that one input channel carries the *true* information about the world and the people in it. Jim might, for example, decide that, when he is faced with the task of determining how to respond to one of his parents who is in a transition from one polarity to another and, therefore, expressing both polarities at once (say, visual and blaming analogically with body movements and gestures, and kinesthetically and placating verbally), he will accept and respond only to messages which he (Jim) receives visually. He, thereby, begins the process of shutting down one of his primary input channels — one of the ways in which he can contact the world and other people — an irreparable loss. Bateson and his colleagues (1972) have dealt with a special case of the kind of choice with which young Jim in our example is faced — the case in which the child makes the best choice in his model at the point in time when he must make a choice to continue to survive — schizophrenia. Apparently, schizophrenia is likely as a choice for children and young adults who are consistently confronted with maximally incongruent communication — the kind, for example, with which Jim's children would be confronted if Jim made this last selection and found a mate who exhibited the same ill-formed polarities.

It follows from the above discussion that the family members — especially the parenting members — will display the same tendencies for non-overlapping representational systems and non-overlapping Satir categories which we discussed in detail in Part II — Incongruency. Both experienced and beginning therapists will find this a powerful organizing principle in their work with family systems. Thus, one of the higher level patterns which the information listed previously will consistently take is that of maximal separation of representational systems and Satir categories.

A second higher level pattern which we have detected again and again in family systems work is the kind of relationship which occurs between the acceptable output channels or modes of expression for family members and the input channels or modes of getting information which they typically use. One way of understanding how this works comes from a consideration of the kinds of experiences that families expect to get from each other in the family system. In the initial stages of family therapy, when asking the family members what it is that each of them hopes for or wants from the therapy, the responses are usually a number of nominalizations; for example, recognition, affection, warmth, love, support, freedom, encouragement, etc. Each of these nominalizations is subject to the Meta-model challenges. The resulting de-nominalizations usually involve a mismatch of input/output channels among the family members who are dissatisfied with what they are receiving at present. We excerpt a section from the early part of a family therapy session:

Therapist: Well, George (a ten-year-old boy), I've heard from all of the family members except you — tell me, what do you want?

George: I want respect.

Matt: (The father in the family) (Smiling broadly) Yes, that I believe.

George: (Explosively) SEE!! That's just what I'm talking about — I don't get any respect from anyone in this family.

Therapist: Wait, George; you sound real angry to me. Can you tell me what just happened with you?

George: I ... I ... oh, never mind; you wouldn't understand anyway.

Therapist: Perhaps not, but try me — did the way you just responded have something to do with something your father did?

George: Yeah, I ask for respect and HE (pointing at his father, Matt) just laughs right out loud, making fun of me.

Matt: That's not true, I didn't ...

Therapist: Be quiet for a moment, Matt. (Turning to George) George, tell exactly what happened with you just then.

George: I asked for respect and my father started making fun of me — just the opposite.

Therapist: George, tell me something — how, specifically, would you know that your father was respecting you?

George: He wouldn't laugh at me — he would watch me when I say things and be serious about it.

Therapist: George, I want to tell you something I noticed and something that I can see right now. Look at your father's face.

George: Yeah, so what?

Therapist: Well, does he look serious to you — does he look like he's taking you seriously right now — like he, maybe, respects you for what you're saying and doing right now?

George: Yeah, you know, he does look like he is.

Therapist: Ask him, George.

George: What? . . . ask him . . . Dad, do you respect me? Are you taking me seriously?

Matt: Yes, son . . . (softly) . . . I'm taking you seriously right now. I respect what you're doing.

George: (Crying softly) I really believe that you do, Dad.

Therapist: I have a hunch right now that Matt has more to say, George; will you take him (indicating Matt) seriously and listen to him?

George: Sure . . .

Matt: Yeah . . . I guess I do have something to say. A minute or so ago when you first said that you wanted respect, George, I smiled and said, "Yes, that I believe" but I guess you only saw the smile and didn't hear what I said (crying quietly), and then, when you became so angry, I suddenly remembered how I never believed my father respected me, and I'm grateful (turning to the therapist) that you helped me straighten this out with George.

Therapist: That's right — a message that's not received the way you intended it is no message at all. Matt, is there some other way that you can show George that you care for him besides telling him that you respect him?

Matt: Huh . . . some other way besides telling him . . . I don't know . . .

Therapist: I have another hunch — that, maybe, there's a rule in this family, maybe a rule that you, Matt, learned in your father's family, that the men in the family don't touch one another to show their affection and love. Do you catch what I mean, Matt?

Matt: ... Wow ... I guess ... I really connected on that one ...

Therapist: Well, maybe it's time for you to try to connect in a new way with your son.

Matt: (Moving slowly and awkwardly at first, then more smoothly, quickly crosses over to George and holds him close.)

In the transcript, we read of the therapist's working first with a family member, George, who receives and acknowledges only part of his father's communication — the smile — and is unaware of the rest — the phrase *Yes, that I believe.* Apparently, at that moment in time, George has only his visual input system operating. The therapist assists George in de-nominalizing the nominalization *respect* by specifying how he would know that his father respected him. Consistent with what just occurred, George specifies the process as one in which he (George) would get visual input *(he would watch me when I . . .).* The therapist now moves to expand the possible ways for George to get that feedback — and does this by making George an active participant in the process of communication by having him ask his father for a verbal reply. This opens up a new output channel as well as a new input channel for George (auditory-verbal). Finally, the therapist goes after one of the rules which limits some of the family members' ability to communicate which he has noticed in the family. Consequently, Matt and George learn a new way of expressing themselves, thereby opening up new input and output channels in which they can make contact.

One very useful way that we have found of organizing our experience in family therapy is to consider rules as limitations imposed by the family system members upon themselves and upon each other. If one family member states that she needs more attention than she is getting from some other specific family member, then, typically, a de-nominalization of *attention* will reveal that the input channels which she is using to detect attention are not capable of detecting the messages in the output system which the other family member is using to try to communicate that attention. For example, the second family member may be giving the first family member his *attention* by listening intently to the first member's speech but, at the same time, failing to make eye contact. The first family member doesn't consider herself to be receiving *attention* unless she has full eye contact with the person to whom she is talking. The channels do not overlap, and the family members end up in pain.

When considered this way, many family rules are restrictions on the input and output channels which may be used to express certain categories of messages. This is a particularly limiting type of deletion — the removal of an entire channel as a means of expression or as a means of making contact. We have usually found that at the base of these channel restrictions are certain fuzzy functions — for example, referring back to Matt and George, it is commonly a *negative* see-feel experience for many males to see males making close physical contact. Another common fuzzy function which occurs in many families is the hear-feel circuits of auditorially expressing anger by yelling or shouting. Many people are amazed to find that they can shout and yell, expressing their anger in this physically non-destructive way, without any of their family members dying or refusing to ever speak to them again.

During this first phase of family therapy, the therapist is alert to identify two things:

(1) The goals (the desired state) that the family wants to achieve;
(2) The present state of the family.

The therapist can precisely determine the first of these by the use of the Meta-model. Simultaneously unfolding before his ears and eyes is a prime example of the family system in process as the family attempts to determine what its goals will be. Here all the skills which make therapy such a demanding and rewarding experience must be used by the therapist to understand the present capabilities and resources as well as the blocks to achieving the desired state in that family system. The therapist's refined ability to detect patterns of congruity and incongruity, to identify representational systems, his understanding of the function of both positive and negative Cause-Effect semantic ill-formedness (and the fuzzy functions which are the neurological basis) are all necessary for an adequate assessment of the family system and the steps necessary for change. Especially important are the higher level patterns of the polarity principle as the primary pairing principle and the translation of rules into restrictions on input and output channels of expressing certain classes of messages in the family system.[3]

In coming to understand these patterns of family interaction, the therapist makes a comparison between the present state of the system and the desired state. Here a clear understanding of the difference and which family rules, representational systems restriction following from the pairing principle, and especially which Cause-Effect semantic ill-formedness (fuzzy function circuits) must be changed in order to help the family to change to achieve the desired state will allow the therapist to act decisively to accelerate the process of change.

EVOLVING THE SYSTEM

Once the patterns of family interaction (rules) have been identified and compared with desired family reference structure (wants), the family therapist then is ready to begin the second phase of a family therapy session, i.e., evolving the system so the rules will not interfere with the needs of the individual members. Closed systems are created by people who are making the best choices in their model of the world, people who are using the processes of human modeling in the best way they know how. But, unfortunately, they are mistaking the map for the territory, and the result is representations which result in rules about how each member of the family system should act (output channels), think (representational systems) and of what they should be aware (input channels). The gap between the wants and needs of the family members and the family patterns and rules is the result of the modeling processes of the family members. For family therapy to be effective, some change in the way family members model (create representations), as well as the rules themselves, must take place. The necessary ingredients for this change have already been presented in *Magic I* and the preceding parts of *Magic II*. However, in Family therapy they must be used in a delicate and special way or the family system will not survive as a system. No one member of the family can be left behind with the old set of rules, and no one member can be outside the rules. The result of alienating a family member in either of two ways will result in a split in the system (divorce, separation, open hostility, or worse). The family therapist must tread this tightrope with the utmost care. However, some simple principles will be provided to make this an easier task. The overall strategy of evolving a family system is to use the three processes of human modeling in such a way that the limits of the family system are expanded.

(1) Again restoring deleted material will be a necessary step. Meta-modeling questioning will serve to provide fuller linguistic communications, and, therefore, representations to listening members. Also, adding new input and output

channels will be an important step. New representational systems will also be important for they are what allow people to communicate in a way which others will understand.

(2) Removal of distortions will constitute a large part of evolving the system, using the Meta-model to de-nominalize linguistically. Relabeling, translating from one representational system to another, and accessing of memories will also play an important role.

(3) Breaking generalizations by Meta-model techniques, comparing models of family members, and especially challenging mind-reading semantic ill-formedness will be necessary steps.

(4) Meta-position moves will also be an effective part of evolving family systems. They can be used to both educate members in more effective forms of communication and at the same time to change patterns of see-feel and hear-feel which result in rigid rules.

If a family therapist can evolve a family system so that feedback is not calibrated, then new patterns of behavior will emerge from all family members as they create richer representations of the shared world in which they live. This will, however, require that members of the family learn that the map is not the territory, at least in some areas of their lives. This is rarely accomplished just by telling anyone, and the focus of the therapist's work is to provide experiences for family members to learn that this point is an undeniable reality, as well as a pleasant one. The pain and hopelessness of those who seek family therapy is evidenced by their presence. They want more than they have, and they do not believe that they have the resources to get it. The truly skilled therapist will have to do more than just provide a solution to the immediate problem. He will have to make the discovery of that solution a pleasant experience, providing patterns of coping that can generalize to other areas of the family's life, at the same time making it possible for every member of the family to be respectable to every other member. Creation of new, negative fuzzy functions will not be nearly as beneficial as making it fun and rewarding to learn new ways of coping. The ideal outcome of family therapy is to create an open system which will be generative in creating new patterns of coping based upon sensory feedback.

Now, let's consider a family interview, piece by piece, and give some meaning to the principles we are presenting here. This is the first time that this family has been interviewed by this therapist. There are four members:

Samuel A.	Husband-father	41	A teacher in high school
Jill A.	Wife-mother	38	Bank Teller
Holly A.	Sister-daughter	16	
Thomas A.	Brother-son	15	

This family "volunteered" to be interviewed as a training demonstration with one of the authors. They had been seen previously two times by another therapist who described them to the author as an impossible group, uncooperative, whom he didn't believe really wanted to be helped until he challenged them to volunteer for the demonstration. When they accepted, he was surprised; he then warned both authors that they might be a bad choice for a demonstration because they were likely to be uncooperative. We chose this transcript for its unique quality of showing just how easily good intentions can be misinterpreted. No other information was given to the therapist before this session at the therapist's request. The family came in: Mother and then father, holding both the children's hands. They sat in the four chairs provided:

Son   Father

Mother   Daughter

The therapist then entered. Introductions were made by the commentator.

Therapist: I am very grateful you could come and be here with me today. I would also like to thank you for being open enough to let those watching share this experience with us so that they might have some new learnings. I also hope that this time can make it possible for all of you (addressing the family) to learn some new things too. I would like to begin by finding out just what those might be. Let me start with you, Samuel. What would you like to come out of this time we have together? What do you hope can happen today?

Samuel: Ummm well, I don't know what will happen.

Therapist: I believe you're right; I don't know either. But what do you *hope* could happen?

Samuel: Oh ... We first went to Dr. P. because of Holly. She kinda got into some trouble and it was recommended that we go to him. We know that she is upset and acting out and her mother is very upset.

Therapist: Let me interrupt you, Samuel. I hear you saying that Holly has done something, and I don't know just what that is. And I also hear you saying, Jill, there has been some pain with this. I would like to know two things: specifically, what trouble did Holly get into, and, second, and most important, just exactly what you want for yourself today.

Samuel: She's been in trouble at school, talking back to teachers and she . . .

Jill: (Interrupting) She's been going through some rebellious stage, and she doesn't *see* how serious this is. She's acting up in every way to *show* everyone how independent she can be, and she just doesn't *see* what she's doing to us and . . .

Therapist: Hold it a minute, Jill. I want to hear about this from you, but first I would like to finish with Samuel. Is that all right with you?

Jill: I guess so.

Samuel: Thanks (sarcastically). I . . . I believe I would like things to *settle down*. Yes, I would like Jill and Holly to *let go of each other's throats*. They bicker, bicker, bicker, and it just keeps getting worse!

Jill: Well, if you . . .

Therapist: Jill . . .

Jill: OK, I'll wait.

Holly: I'll bet you will.

Jill: Now you'll . . .

Therapist: Hold it. We have been here only a few minutes and already I see and hear that you have some pain with each other. I would very much like to see, Jill and Holly, if we can't find a way to make things better for both of you. But, first, I need to know some things from each of you. Would you be willing to let each member of the family speak, no matter what they say, so that each of you can have a turn without being interrupted? (They all nod affirmatively.) Thank you. Samuel?

Samuel: That's really the *crust* of it. I just get so *irritated* when they start that crap. I would like it to stop.

Therapist: Samuel, is there anything else you would really like for you, some hope you have?

Samuel: Yes. I would like the fighting to stop; I would also like more *affection* from my wife. She's . . . well, she doesn't act much like she used to anymore.

Therapist: Jill, what do you hope can happen here; what changes do you hope for?

Jill: I hope that somehow things can be *cleared up* with Holly before she really makes a big mistake.

Therapist: What things do you see as needing to be cleared up, Jill?

Jill: Holly's behavior.

Therapist: What behavior, specifically?

Jill: She . . . Well, two things. She needs to *show* some respect and *show* some sense of responsibility.

Therapist: Jill, could you say just how you would like to see Holly show some respect to you?

Jill: She disobeys me, stays out too late, and is never at home to help clean the house and do things like that. We both work and she should help me with the house; you know, *show* some responsibility. Her room *looks* like a pigsty and . . .

Therapist: Jill, have you ever seen a pigsty?

Jill: Well, no, but you know what I mean.

Therapist: I would like to hear, because I have a difficult time imagining her room covered with mud and corn cobs (all laughing).

Jill, I hear and see that you have a lot of concern about Holly and that maybe you also need some help from her. I would like to find a way for you to have those things. Let's see what happens. Let me check now with Holly.

The therapist continued in this fashion around the room to both Holly and Thomas. Holly wanted freedom from her mother. She called her a nag, a worry-wart, and a tyrant. She also wanted to "see her mother get off daddy's back." Thomas claimed he wanted nothing and just came because his mother dragged him, but would like the "yelling to stop." He said, "I feel sometimes like it's open warfare at home, everybody pounding on everyone else." When the therapist asked him what he wanted just for himself he said, "Quiet."

In the above transcript there is enough information provided, even with the deletion of part of the transcript, to begin to notice some patterns in this family's behavior which will help to make positive change from this experience. First is most highly valued representational systems. Samuel is primarily kinesthetic-placating; Jill, visual-blaming; Holly, visual-blaming; Thomas, kinesthetic-placating. The result is a stable but rigid family system. Even in the first few minutes of this session, the family members have begun to respond quickly with what could be mistaken as bad behavior. They could be termed uncooperative, but that would be inaccurate. Quite the contrary, they responded in a way which provided just the information necessary for family therapy to be useful and effective. The therapist has elecited a great deal of information by matching his predicates to those of his clients, asking Jill questions phrased with visual predicates such as *show clearly*, etc. This session lasted some two and one-half hours and constitutes some hundred and sixty pages of written material. For that reason, only portions of it will be presented. These portions are supplied to demonstrate various aspects of how family systems are evolved. In the first twenty-five minutes the following patterns were revealed.

Samuel *"felt"* uncared for by Jill; he longed for affection, and also desired to have his family be more *in touch* with each other's needs. He also felt his wife didn't respect his wishes; she kept her job in spite of his requests that she quit and stay home with the family and take care of the house. And he felt that she shouldn't go out with the girls to bars without him. Jill *"saw"* things quite differently. She thought her husband was too jealous and couldn't *"see how silly that is."* She also wanted him to be stricter with Holly. She said he *"just doesn't look at* what is happening right *in front* of him." She also said, *"Clearly,* Holly has got to *shape up"* and that "Holly should be more like her brother." Holly thought that her father should stand up to Jill. "He just lets her *push* everyone around; I watch that and, well, not me." "I show her she can't get away with that, not with me." Thomas "felt sick when they fight all the time." He just wanted to run away and hide.

Let us now examine the reference structures desired by the family and see what kind of evolving will be necessary for this family to find some new choices which are more satisfying.

In order for the members of this family to achieve their desired aims, certain changes will be necessary. If Jill and Holly are to find any connections with each other, and if Jill is to have her "image" of Holly clarified and vice versa, they will have to learn two facets of their map's not being the territory. First, that the incongruency of their communication prevents their desired outcomes, e.g., Jill's messages of being concerned about Holly are communicated in a blaming way, a way that sounds critical, not concerned. Jill's words do not match her tone of voice and body gestures. Incongruent communication is the normal way of exchanging messages in this family. Even when Samuel said he desired more affection from his wife, his tones and words were not matching; they conveyed other messages which were interpreted by Jill as criticisms about her behavior. Communication by members of this family seemed to be, in itself, a risk. Any comment was sure to be a criticism of some other family member. They were all calibrated to receive bad messages, and, thus, every message was construed to be a bad one. All members of this family system believed in their mind-reading abilities; every misinterpretation was then turned into a hear-feel. Family members would have to learn both to communicate their own messages and to receive messages from other members. Secondly, actions of the family members were construed to have specific meanings (see-feels) which, if the members were to have more communication with each other, would have to be changed. Mistaking the actions of Jill, Holly would immediately move to protect herself. Holly also has mistaken the map for the territory and has calibrated her sight. During the session, Jill reached for Holly's hand in what appeared to the therapist to be an attempt to become more connected and an attempt by Jill to develop some kinesthetic input. Holly pulled back and accused her mother of trying to hold her to make her look like a little child.

The rules go something like this:
   Don't listen, it will just hurt anyway.
   Don't bother to say anything nice because no one will hear.
   Don't ask because you shouldn't be selfish, and you won't get anything anyway.
   Don't touch if anybody else is watching; they'll see-feel, especially Mother.
   Be strong, not yourself, or you'll get hurt.

These rules were not developed by people who were trying to create pain for each other but by people who were doing the best they could with their particular patterns of incongruent communication and fuzzy functions. The following excerpts are from the part of the interview which dealt with evolving the system. They have been added to demonstrate the pattern of using all of the techniques presented in *Magic I* and so far in *Magic II* for the purpose of evolving a system.

   Therapist: What, exactly, do you want for Holly? Jill, what would you like changed in your relationship with her?
   Jill: (Critical tone) I just want her to be happy and to show

her how to not make the same mistakes that I did. I want her to see I am really trying.

Therapist: As you say that Jill, I can believe that you really do want more for Holly, but your tone of voice is harsh as you say these things about wanting to help her and be closer, and I'm wondering if Holly doesn't hear your message as something like: "You're not doing anything right; you never do. You don't see how much I'm doing for you" (exaggerated, blaming tone and comical gestures). Is that what it's like when you hear your mother speak like this?

Holly: Yes, she always claims to know what's right for everybody.

Therapist: It must be a terrible task to keep tabs on billions of people in this world. Does she really claim to know what's best for everybody or just you?

Holly: Well, lots of people.

Therapist: Jill, did you know that Holly didn't understand your message as one of trying to help, and took it rather as more criticism?

Jill: Sort of . . .

Therapist: Would you like to find a new way to communicate your desire to help her, and to ask for help from her?

Jill: Yes, I would.

Therapist: Holly, as you hear your mother say that she would like to find a new way with you, I wonder if you also would like to find something new with her?

Holly: I think she just wants to find some way of telling me to do things that will make me do them.

Therapist: You believe that to be true?

Holly: Yes.

Therapist: Would you like to find out if it's true?

Holly: Yes.

Therapist: Then, would you ask her? I think people in this family spend a lot of time guessing what other people mean, and I also think that they guess wrong a lot of the time. Let's find out. Ask her now.

There are two interesting patterns in the following section. First, in the comment on Jill's incongruity, the therapist is trying to demonstrate to Jill that her messages are not received at all like she intends them to be. This opens up the possibility of discovering better ways of communicating, at the same time demonstrating what those ways are; in this case, auditory feedback instead of calibration. Secondly, the therapist is making a direct challenge on mind-reading semantic ill-formedness, first demonstrating that it has happened, and then offering a new alternative, asking. This is also the first step in developing a new representational system which can be shared by both Jill and Holly.

> *Holly:* Do you just want to find a way to make me do things?
> *Jill:* No, I just don't want to be locked out; I worry so about you.
> *Therapist:* What did you hear, Holly?
> *Holly:* She still thinks I can't take care of myself.
> *Therapist:* Jill, did you say, or do you think, that Holly can't take care of herself?
> *Jill:* No, I didn't say that. I . . . I . . . think she can, but . . .
> *Therapist:* But what?
> *Jill:* Well, she is only 16.
> *Therapist:* Only 16?

This is a good example of how the process of comparing models can take place. The next step made by the therapist continues this theme, by having these two visual women use their most highly valued representational system to compare their models even further.

> *Therapist:* Jill and Holly, I would like you to try something to see if maybe we can't clear up some of this a little. Would you both come here? Now, close your eyes and just make a picture of your mother, and, Jill, make a picture of Holly. Look at it closely, and, without opening your eyes, what do you see, Jill?
> *Jill:* My little girl, dressed pretty and . . .
> *Holly:* You always see me as a little girl.
> *Therapist:* Just close your eyes, Holly; wait and see what happens. Holly, what do you see?
> *Holly:* Mother, pointing her finger, looking disgusted and angry again.
> *Therapist:* Now, while you keep your eyes closed, I would like to tell you what I see, and what I hear. I see Holly, sixteen years old growing into an adult. And I hear, Jill — you still have Holly saddled with some picture you have about how she used to be. I also see Jill as a mother who is trying to find a way to be connected with her daughter, and, Holly, you have saddled her with a picture of some controlling monster. I think you don't know each other. Would you

like to open your eyes and really meet each other, maybe for the first time in years?

Jill: (Beginning to sob) Yes, yes I would.

Therapist: Holly, I see you looking surprised. Holly, maybe this is a new you.

Holly: I don't believe that we'll . . . (starts to sob a little).

Therapist: What don't you believe?

Holly: That she . . .

Therapist: Ask her.

Holly: Could you really see me as a person, as . . .

Jill: Yes, but it's scary.

Therapist: Could you say what's scary, Jill?

Jill: You're growing up and I'm afraid I'll lose you.

Therapist: You can't lose her until you have her; do you really have her yet?

Jill: No, but I want to.

Once these two had learned that their models of each other were outmoded, they could begin to find new ways to communicate with each other. They have begun to learn that mind reading sets limits and puts walls between them. They continued, with the help of the therapist, to make a new contract about how they would interact, learning check-out communication.

This next excerpt is from about twenty minutes later when the therapist changed the focus from Jill and Holly to Jill and Samuel. Asking Jill if, now that she had some new connections with Holly, she would like to find some new ways with Samuel.

Jill: (Looking at Samuel, now responding to the therapist's question) I want you to not watch over me, not always ask where I've been and who I saw, and not try and make me quit work.

Samuel: I don't anymore; you've bitched and bitched and I just don't . . .

Jill: Oh, come on; you give those looks, and coy questions . . .

Samuel: Shit; you imagine . . .

Therapist: Wait a minute, you're slipping off. What, exactly, do you want from Jill?

Samuel: I would like her to be more affectionate, and . . .

Therapist: Easy now, slow down. More affectionate, how?

Samuel: I want her to kiss me and, you know, but she always says not here, not in front of the kids, not now . . .

Therapist: Jill, do you have some clear idea what Samuel is talking about?

Jill: I think so; he wants to paw me and I believe that privately that sorta thing is OK but not in front of the kids.

Therapist: What do you think would happen if your children saw Samuel and you being affectionate?

Jill: Well ... (pause) ... it would make them uncomfortable.

Therapist: How do you know that?

Jill: I see them when he does it; I see their faces.

Therapist: You're guessing again; would you like to find out if that's true?

Jill: I don't know.

Therapist: If you don't know, guess.

Jill: Holly, does it?

Holly: No, it bothers me when I see you push him away; I think you don't love him.

Jill: Oh ...

Thomas: Yeah, I always thought you didn't like dad; sometimes it felt creepy when you ...

Therapist: Ummmm guess you were wrong on that one too, Jill. Is there anything else that stops you from being more affectionate with Samuel?

Jill: (Sighs) Yes, I guess there is; I feel cowed by him.

Therapist: How?

Jill: He prys into my life, and ...

Samuel: I thought we were married.

Therapist: Samuel, does being married mean that you don't have any privacy or have your private activities?

Samuel: No, she has lots of them, but when I try to get involved in any way, she says I'm invading her space.

Therapist: Jill, what I hear Samuel saying, correct me if I'm wrong, Samuel, is that he sees you doing a lot of things without him and he doesn't see you doing things with him. This sort of looks like you don't want him or need him. And any time he shows an interest you see him as prying.

Jill: No, I see him asking about where I've been, what did I do, who did I see ...

Therapist: Hold it, Jill; were you deliberately trying to pry into Holly's affairs?

Jill: Ah, no, not deliberately, I mean.

Therapist: Is it possible that maybe this is another example of the same thing, only this time you're the one who feels invaded?

Jill: I guess it's possible.

Therapist: Do you think it's more than possible?

Jill: Yes.

Therapist: Samuel, are you trying to invade Jill's space or are you asking for some attention?

Samuel: I want some attention.

Therapist: Jill, do you know anything about wanting attention and not getting it? Do you know how desperately you can try and how your messages can be misunderstood? Isn't that just what happened with Holly?

Jill: I guess it is.

Therapist: Would you two pull your chairs over here, facing each other. That's right.

In the preceding excerpt there are some interesting patterns. (1) The way the therapist translates from one representational system to another, taking Samuel's kinesthetic predicates and communicating his message to Jill in visual predicates. This assists these two people in sharing information that otherwise could not be shared. At the same time it directly challenges mind reading. (2) The way the therapist re-labels the problem between Jill and Samuel to show them it has the same formal characteristics as the problem between Jill and Holly. Since Jill has this experience, she can switch the referential indices of Samuel's experience to her own, thus making a connection that would not otherwise be possible. (3) The therapist is also presenting himself as a model of how the same message can be communicated congruently, with the outcome being the desired reference structure. This puts Samuel in a meta-position with respect to his own communication, first by his attempt's being misinterpreted and then, next, by hearing and seeing both his polarities' being communicated congruently, with the result being understanding. This offers him a new choice about how to convey his messages, at the same time offering Jill a new choice about how she receives them.

Therapist: I would like to spend a few minutes now trying to see if it is possible for me to teach you to make some meaning between you. What I want to do is to teach you about really hearing each other and really seeing each other as you are. Jill, would you begin now? Just take each other's hands, and, looking each other in the eyes, Jill would you ask for what you want for yourself in a way which you believe that Samuel can really hear? Samuel, just listen.

Jill: Please let me have my own space without being bitter or making snide remarks or giving those looks.

Therapist: Samuel, what I hear from Jill is that she wants space, which she already has but in a new way, in a way that she feels is really all right with you. She wants you to grasp that she feels bad inside when she gets non-verbal or verbal messages that you don't approve of her and what she does. Do you understand that?

Samuel: I think so, but she hasn't left anything for me. She (Samuel points to Jill), you haven't left anything for me; I feel pushed away all of the time.

Therapist: Jill, can you see how it is for Samuel to see you enjoying doing things by yourself, without him, and not to see you do things with him that he values?

Samuel: I also don't want to feel that it's wrong for me to be interested in what you do.

Therapist: Do you know about being interested in another person and having that person, Jill, think that you're invading her space?

Jill: I do.

Therapist: I guess what you're saying, Samuel, is that you want Jill to approve of what you do, is that right?

Samuel: What?

Therapist: I said, it sounds to me like you want Jill to approve of your interest in her, to approve of your affection, to approve of your company, in the same way that you, Jill, want Samuel to approve of your taking time for yourself and working. And, in the same way, you, Jill, want Holly to approve of your interest in her. Is this what's really going on here?

Samuel: I never looked at it that way.

Therapist: Well, maybe this is a new way of understanding things for you. How about you, Jill?

Jill: I think you're right.

Therapist: Would you take each other's hands for a moment and let your eyes close. Now, I would like you to think back to when you first decided this guy was for you, Jill, and when you, Samuel, first decided that Jill was the girl for you. Now, without saying a word, let your eyes open and see if you see that person still here in front of you. Some years have passed; you both learned some new things. What do you see, Jill?

Jill: I feel like I haven't looked at him for a long time.

Therapist: Jill, promise me that you won't forget to look in this way, and, if you should, that you'll just sit down like you are now, even if you're in the middle of a fight, and

look in this way. Will you do that?
Jill: I'll try.
Samuel: May I remind you?
Jill: I wish you would.

The preceding transcript offers some other valuable patterns for evolving a family system. (1) The therapist re-labeled the unfulfilled needs of the family members as really being the same. This is very easy when you consider that they are the result of the same set of rules and the same system. (2) The result of this was that Samuel "saw" things differently; he is building a new representational system. Also, memories connected with feeling were accessed to help Jill recover the kinesthetic representations she felt for Samuel at another point in their life. These two have begun to build bridges between them. They are beginning to share representational systems. The most unused representational system is auditory and offers a vast resource for developing connections. Also, new input channels are being developed; auditory input in the past has been almost totally ignored by this family. Now it becomes a valid way of receiving and validating information. Since no member of a family system should be left out, the therapist now moved to build some new bridges for Thomas, who has watched and listened in amazement to the preceding two hours.

Therapist: I haven't forgotten you, Thomas, or is it Tom?
Tom: Tom. I've never seen them like this.
Therapist: Like what, Tom?
Tom: So nice to each other; will it last?
Therapist: Would you like to find out? Ask someone here.
Tom: Mom, is this gonna last?
Jill: Not all the time dear, but a lot of the time. We have to learn lots more before it will be like this all of the time. Do you understand that?
Tom: Sure; nobody can be good all of the time; it's too hard.
Therapist: Is there anyone you would like to feel closer to?
Tom: Everyone, I guess.
Therapist: Good, because I noticed something about this family. There is very little touching going on here. You all must get skin hungry. Everyone needs some hugs and that kind of thing. Would you let me show you one more thing which I believe you all could share? It's a simple thing Virginia Satir, who was my teacher, uses with families she sees, to help them to get used to touching each other more often. Would you be willing?

This session closed with a family huddle, and a request that the family practice this huddle at least once a day. As a review of their new learning, they concluded the session with each member telling the others what he had learned. The family then departed, saying their good-byes to the therapist. After they had left, a small piece of paper was found on Holly's chair. On it was written, "Thank you again. H."

META-TACTIC FOR EVOLVING A FAMILY SYSTEM

The last section provided you with an example of how a family system is evolved. We will now present a series of tactics to accomplish this task. However, we do remind you that the overall strategy should remain constant when employing these tactics. That is, evolving a family system implies that, after comparing the relationship between input/output channels and the resulting fuzzy functions, the family rules are compared with the reference structure desired by the family members. The evolution of the system will require first, changing those areas of the family members' models which are impoverished in some way which prohibits the evolving of the desired reference structure. The family members must learn that their map is not the territory, and that the changes are more acceptable than the rules which prevented them. This can be accomplished in the following ways:

COMPARING MODELS

1. *The use of Meta-model questions* to elicit a full representation of each member's model of the world. This allows auditory input to be maximal for each member, at the same time providing the information necessary to produce change.

2. *Meta-comments on incongruency in communication.* I hear you say that you are communicating *caring* but you *sound angry* and *look angry*. These comments allow a member to understand how his messages are misconstrued by the others and also allow the other members to better understand how they misconstrued the messages in the first place.

3. *Challenging mind reading* is a most essential part of evolving a family system. It allows clients to develop auditory feedback, at the same time giving them an experience in just how much their map is not the territory.

PERMUTATIONS OF REPRESENTATIONS

1. *Switching representational systems* gives a member a chance to describe his experience which would normally be unacceptable, using auditory output in an acceptable way.

2. *Re-labeling* has two parts. First, the re-labeling of any behavior which has a negative see-feel or a negative hear-feel by describing the polarity function, and in this way making the unacceptable acceptable.

> *Therapist:* How, specifically, does she make you angry?
>
> *Husband:* She's always nagging at me to stay home with her.
>
> *Therapist:* You don't realize that her nagging shows just how much she really cares for you. She wouldn't nag if it weren't important. She is really giving a caring message about just how important you are to her. Isn't that right, W?
>
> *Wife:* Well, yes.
>
> *Therapist:* So, when she nags you, you have a choice: to respond in your old way or to appreciate just how much she really cares, and then you could take her nagging as a love message.

The second form of re-labeling is equating, as shown in the transcript about Jill, Holly, Samuel, and Thomas. Jill learned that her requests deserved approval, just as did Samuel's.

3. *Referential index shift* occurs when the negative experiences of one family member are understood by another, by "imagining yourself with (the same problem)."

4. *Accessing memories* is a technique used to recover positive fuzzy functions and to restore them to the family system.

5. *Translating from one representational system to another* allows clients to better understand each other's representations, at the same time giving them a model to develop new ways of communicating auditorially.

META-POSITION MOVES

1. *Meta-questions* such as,

How do you feel about feeling X?

allow the members to express both polarities and allow the listening members greater access to information formerly not received since it was never expressed auditorially.

> *Husband:* I feel angry about that.
> *Therapist:* And how do you feel about feeling angry at your wife?
> *Husband:* I don't like it.
> *Therapist:* Did you know, W, that M did not like getting angry at you?

2. *Sculpturing* is the technique of placing family members in physical positions in relationship to one another which represent the formal characteristics of their communication (see Satir, 1973).

3. *The therapist as a model* provides a necessary reference structure for members to experience effective and congruent communication which will result in the nominalization of the desired reference structure.

4. *The addition of any new representational system* or input or output channel is a most desired activity. This is most easily accomplished by creating tasks which require their use.

All of the above tactics provide a vehicle for evolving a family system. Additional reading is suggested in the Bibliography of *Magic I.*

INTEGRATION OF NEW CHOICES AND PATTERNS — CONSOLIDATION OF META-POSITION

The goal in family therapy is to assist the family system in evolving from the state in which they are first encountered in therapy to the state which they have identified as being desirable. In evolving a family system in the second phase of family system therapy, the therapist is careful to move only as quickly as all members of the family are able to respond. From a system point of view and from the point of view of having a maximally beneficial effect in working with the family, the therapist's objective is to assist the family in evolving to the identified desirable state, while simultaneously changing the coping patterns so that other disturbances, not identified initially by the family members but which might subsequently arise, can be dealt with in a creative way by the family itself. In system terms, this is known as *morphogenesis.* The type of system which is characteristically morphogenetic is the open system — a system which is responsive to its environment and readily adapts itself to disturbances in an acceptable and creative manner.

While an open system is the most desirable outcome of family therapy, this is a difficult goal to achieve. Furthermore, family therapy is conducted in the real world with real time constraints on both the family and the therapist. Consistent with the principle of operating with the family as an organism, the therapist must employ a set of techniques which will assist the family between sessions in consolidating the advances made during the therapy sessions, or the family will achieve only limited goals which fall short of the ideal of a completely open system whose members have a maximum amount of choice. Thus, for example, at the end of each family therapy session, the family will return to its home and cope as best it can until the next scheduled session. In order to insure the maintenance of the family as an intact unit between sessions, the therapist may use one of the following techniques. Common to each of these techniques is the fact that it is designed to assist the family members in being aware of the new choices and new coping patterns which they have evolved with the therapist during their session. There are two general categories of these techniques:

1. *Homework assignments* — exercises given to members of the family for them to perform to give them practice in their new choices and skills;
2. *Signals* which will constitute an effective interception of old and destructive patterns should these reassert themselves.

Homework is essentially designed to give family members practice in using their new choices and skills. These are most often connected, in our experience, with the exercise of new input and output channels. For example, in a family in which, traditionally, family members accepted a rule which identified touching among family members as a negative see-feel, a useful exercise of their new choices and patterns would be scheduled massage in which all family members participate. As another example, in a family in which verbal communication was traditionally non-existent, during a specified period of time each family member would talk about some part of his recent experiences or current interests. Homework, to be maximally effective, should use precisely the new patterns learned in the therapy session and should provide a scheduled occasion for family members to exercise exactly the new choices most recently developed in the therapeutic context. Here, the family itself will be the best judge of how to incorporate these new dimensions into the ongoing flow of their life as a family. Allowing the responsibility of creating these homework assignments to rest with the family itself insures that the family will, in fact, carry out the homework assignment and that it will be appropriate in the non-therapeutic context. In addition, the process of developing exercises and deciding on how to use them is an excellent experience in which family members come to appreciate their own skills and those of the other family members.

The second category of techniques to assist the family in consolidating meta-position is that of intercept *signals*. Typically, in a family who has come to therapy for assistance in changing its unsatisfactory patterns of interaction, the patterns the family members have developed which they are attempting to change are initially so strong that a lapse into an old pattern by a single member of the family is sufficient to draw in the other family members — and the gains made by the family are temporarily undermined. To prevent this from occurring, family therapists develop a set of cues or signals which will allow family members to detect and signal other family members that an old and unsatisfactory pattern of interaction is beginning. All of the considerations presented in Part II on incongruity work, in the section on polarity signals, are valid here. For example, we favor kinesthetic cues; these seem to work particularly well when the patterns to be counteracted are patterns which involve the fuzzy functions which are the basis of Cause-Effect semantic ill-formedness. Since the typical fuzzy function involved here is a see-feel or a hear-feel, kinesthetic cues are easily detected. In fact, often in our work with changing fuzzy functions, we give a graded series of signals in which the initial signal is kinesthetic and the subsequent cues move out to the associated representational system. For example, with a see-feel circuit, the initial cue might be a reversal of breathing; the final cue, the actual visual input. In this way, the family members learn as a matter of course to see-see — a valuable learning in and of itself.

Another effective signal, especially in families with small

children who as yet are less skilled in verbalizations than other family members, is sculpturing. Sculpturing is a form of meta-commenting without requiring verbal skill, as it makes use of body postures by the person initiating the signal and the visual input channels by the person receiving the signal.

As with the homework exercises, the family should be involved maximally in the planning and rehearsal of intercept signals. With these cues, it is particularly important to consider the most dependable input and output channels available to all family members.

FOOTNOTES FOR PART IV

1. In our experience, the breaking up of a family system may, in some circumstances, be the most beneficial outcome for the family members in terms of their ability to change and grow — thus, the most acceptable outcome rather than the least acceptable. One case of this which will be clear to the reader is that of the family system with an identified patient schizophrenic who is struggling to free himself from the patterns of family interaction in which he is trapped.

2. This seems to us to be the basic pattern of the traditional psychotherapeutic phenomenon of transference, negative transference and counter transference.

3. R. D. Laing (see pp. 104-124, *The Politics of the Family and Other Essays*, Vintage Books, 1972) has an interesting discussion of rules and meta-rules. As far as we can determine, his meta-rules are the basis for a person's actually blocking an entire input or output channel. For example, the person begins with a rule, say,

Do not notice (visually) incongruity.

Then, after some period of time, his behavior becomes congruent with the meta-rule,

Do not notice that you do not notice (visually) incongruity.

PART V

Formal Notation

In *The Structure of Magic I,* we presented an explicit verbal model for therapy. This model is designed to teach the therapist how to hear and respond to the form of the client's surface structures. The content may vary infinitely; the form which the client uses allows the therapist to respond in a systematic pattern that assists the client in changing. Specifically, by responding to the form of the client's surface structures, the therapist quickly comes to understand the client's model of the world, its impoverishing limitations and the modeling processes which the client typically uses to construct his models. Listening to and responding to the client in terms of the Meta-model distinctions allow the therapist to identify the techniques he will use to assist the client in changing.

The Meta-model which we presented in *Magic I* has a number of useful distinctions. As we stated in that volume, these distinctions themselves fall into natural groupings or meta-patterns of the Meta-model distinctions. We have found it useful in organizing our experience both in therapy and in our Therapist Training Seminars to divide the Meta-model distinctions into three classes:

(a) Gathering information;
(b) Identifying the limits of the client's model;
(c) Specifying the techniques to be used for change.

FUNCTIONS

Formally, functions are rules of association or rules which specify a connection between a member or members of one group (called the domain) and those of another (called the range). To use a commonplace function as an example, consider the mother function. The mother function can be understood as the rule of association which, given any human being, specifies who that individual's mother is. Notice what is involved here: two sets of humans: *Set I,* the set of all human beings, and *Set II,* the set of all mothers, and a rule of association, *f,* which specifies which person has which mother. Using the standard functional notations, we have:

(a) f (Set I)————→(Set II)

or

(b) f (Set I, Set II)

In words, the visual representations above may be translated as:

(a) The function *f* associates (maps) members of Set I with (onto or into) members of Set II.
(b) The function *f* specifies ordered pairs whose first member is from Set I and whose second member is from Set II.

Notice that the two sets whose connection is specified by the function may have members in common — in this example, all the members of Set II are also members of Set I, but all of the male members of Set I are not members of Set II.

Functional notation is simply a way of representing visually the regularities in our experience. If we know that, when we encounter some situation which has occurred repeatedly in our experience and that each time in the past when we have done such and such an act, the situation has changed to some new situation, then we typically develop a rule of association or a *function* to express this regularity and communicate it to others:

ACT (situation 1)————————→(situation 2)

or

ACT (situation 1, situation 2)

All that is required is that we be able to identify the sets involved and the way in which members of one of the sets are linked with members of the other set. One way, then, of representing the process of change in therapy which occurs at the highest level of patterning is:

Therapist (Client state$_i$)————————→(Client state$_j$)

We have already employed the notion of function earlier in our work — the Meta-model, for example. To reformulate it in the visual notation presented here requires that we be explicit about the sets which are being mapped. We proceed by example. The client says,

I'm scared.

This Surface Structure is the outcome of a linguistic process called a derivation. One of the principal research domains of transformational linguistics is derivations — the relationship between full linguistic representations — the set of Deep Structures — and expressed linguistic representations — the set of Surface Structures. Using our functional notation,

transformational syntax (Deep Structure)——►(Surface Structures)

or

transformational syntax (Deep Structures, Surface Structures)

In the specific case of the Surface Structure *I'm scared*, there is a Deep Structure with which it is associated, namely,

> *SCARE [someone/thing, me]*

If we let the symbol *d* represent the linguistic process of deletion, we may represent the entire process through which the client has gone by:

> d (SCARE [someone/thing, me])——————►(I'm scared)

or

> d (SCARE [someone/thing, me], I'm scared)

As we mentioned previously, functional notation is a way of visually representing regularities in our experience, requiring only that we be able to identify explicitly the sets involved and the rule of correspondence or function which links members of one set with those of the other. The notation, being formal, is independent of content — in fact, sets of functions may, themselves, constitute the sets which are being associated by the same rules of correspondence. When considering the relationship between sets of functions, there is one special relationship which has been distinguished by mathematicians. These are called inverse functions. Again, we proceed by example.

(I)

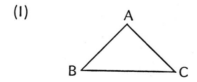

Now consider all the ways in which you could turn (rotate) this triangle in two dimensions. You could, for example, rotate it as follows:

(II)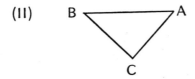

Suppose we now consider a rotation of the original triangle by moving it 120° to the right. The result would be:

(III)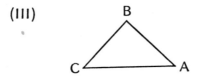

Or, using a related notation,

rotation r-120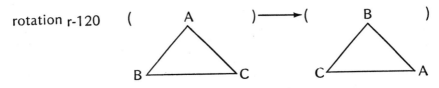

Or, again, using the functional notation we presented previously,

$$R_{r\text{-}120} \quad (I) \longrightarrow (III)$$

Now return to the original triangle (I) and consider the result of a rotation of 240° to the left. You will notice that the outcome of $R_{l\text{-}240}$ is identical to $R_{r\text{-}120}$. Thus, $R_{l\text{-}240}$ and $R_{r\text{-}120}$ are inverse functions.

Or, symbolically, if $R_{l\text{-}240}$ is f, then $R_{r\text{-}120}$ is f^{-1}

In these examples, we see that the effect of some functions can be reversed by other functions. When this occurs, the second is said to be the inverse of the first. This same patterning occurs in the therapeutic context.

Now, let us return to a consideration of the use of the Meta-model by the therapist. Using the same example of the Surface Structure,

I'm scared.

the Meta-model challenge by the therapist to Surface Structures such as *I'm scared,* when presented by the client, is:

Scared of whom/what?

Notice that the therapist takes as input the Surface Structure which contains the deletion and demands the deleted part. Another way of representing this process is by stating that the Meta-model challenge is a demand on the part of the therapist for the client to perform the inverse operation; in symbols, then:

$$d^{-1} \text{ (I'm scared)} \longrightarrow (\text{SCARE [someone/thing, me]})$$

and then report the result to the therapist.

GATHERING INFORMATION

In order to act effectively in assisting the client, the therapist must come to an understanding of the client's model and the modeling processes which the client uses to organize his experience. The first set of questions or challenges from the Meta-model based on the form of the client's Surface Structures involves the Meta-model distinctions:

> *Deletion;*
> *Lack of referential index;*
> *Unspecified verbs;*
> *Nominalizations.*

The formal characteristic which links each of these distinctions and its corresponding Meta-model challenges is that the challenge is the inverse of the Meta-model distinction which has been violated.

Parallel to the deletion example, when the therapist detects a Surface Structure representation which includes a noun phrase without a referential index — that is, the client's modeling performance in going from Reference Structure to Deep Structure results in the loss of a referential index — the Meta-model challenge is to demand the inverse modeling process. Thus, the exchange:

> *Client:* People scare me.
> *Therapist:* Who, specifically, scares you?

or, in symbolic form: *Client* (r) *Therapist* [*Client* (r^{-1})]

The remaining two distinctions and their associated Meta-model challenges are also inverses and have a parallel symbolic representation:

Unspecified Verbs:
  Client: My father scares me. Client (v)
  Therapist: How, specifically, does he scare you?
    Therapist [Client (v^{-1})]

and

Nominalizations:
  Client: I want respect. Client (n)
  Therapist: Whom do you want to respect you?
    Therapist [Client (n^{-1})]

Thus, in the first phase of therapeutic work — gathering information — the formal generalization is that the therapist's response is to demand that the client perform the inverse linguistic modeling operation. Letting the Greek Symbol $\propto$ represent the class of the four Meta-model distinctions specified by the symbols:

  d, r, v, and n

then the generalization is:

  Client: $\propto$
  Therapist [*Client* $(\propto^{-1})$]

Within this group, there are two other relations which we wish to point out. First, the r and v processes and their associated Meta-model challenges r^{-1} and v^{-1} are identical processes except for the domain (the set of things to which they apply) over which they are defined. The process r maps (associates with) nouns with referential indices into nouns without referential indices, while the process v maps verbs which are relatively specified into less specified verbs. The processes r^{-1} and v^{-1} are the inverse mappings:

r^{-1} (noun phrase without referential index)$\rightarrow$(noun phrase with referential index)

v^{-1} (verb relatively unspecified) $\longrightarrow$ (verb relatively more specified)

Thus, the domain of the functions r and r^{-1} is noun phrases and the domain of the v and v^{-1} is verbs.

Secondly, the first three distinctions are involved in producing the fourth — in other words, n and n^{-1} are complex functions which factor into the first three processes, plus a category shift. In the course of the nominalization process, the linguistic representation shifts from that of a predicate to a noun representation, from a process representation to an event representation. Thus, the client goes from a Deep Structure representation:

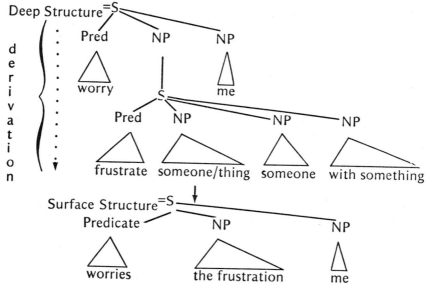

that is, the Surface Structure representation:

The frustration worries me. Client (n)

The therapist responds with the Meta-model challenge:

Whose frustrating whom worries you? Therapist [Client (n^{-1})]

One pattern of learning which we have noticed again and again in our training seminars is that people learning the Meta-model have a tendency to become caught in a cycle; they often describe their experience "as going around and around and getting nowhere." This cycle occurs when the therapist remains in these first-level patterns in the processes d, r, v, n and the inverse patterns; d^{-1}, r^{-1}, v^{-1}, and n^{-1}. The reader will notice that this is a common pattern at other levels of structure. In polarity work, for example, if the therapist plays the opposite polarity — the inverse at that level of patterning — then the client will continue to be stuck in the dominant polarity or the polarity which is the inverse of the one the therapist is playing.

In order to break this vicious cycle, the therapist refines his ability to hear and challenges the distinctions which are characteristic of the next phase.

IDENTIFYING THE LIMITS OF THE CLIENT'S MODEL(S)

In the second phase of therapy, the most useful Meta-model distinctions are those which identify the limits of the model which the client is using to organize his ongoing experience. Specifically, these include:

> modal operators
> semantic ill-formedness
>> Cause-Effect
>> Mind-reading
>> Lost Performative

When the client uses Surface Structures which include a modal operator of possibility or necessity, he is, literally, identifying the limits of his model. His communication is a direct language representation of the portion of his model which has inadequate choices, or, more often, no choice at all. Notice that the Meta-model challenges to modal operators are requests for the client to fill in a larger level deletion while presupposing the semantically ill-formed modeling process of Cause-Effect. For example:

> *Client:* I can't leave home.
> *Therapist:* What would happen if you left home?

or

> *Therapist:* What stops you from leaving home?

In the first therapist's Meta-model response, the client's statement is accepted as a Cause of something, and the client is requested to specify what the Effect would be of doing what is claimed to be impossible. In the second case, the client's statement is accepted as an Effect and the client is requested to specify what the Cause of this supposed impossibility is. In both cases, the client's statement is accepted by the therapist as a portion of a semantically ill-formed Cause-Effect relationship (as either X or Y in the following form):

$$X \quad \text{causes} \quad Y$$

and the client is requested to supply the material which has been deleted in the mapping from Reference Structure to Deep Structure. Thus, the d and d^{-1} patterns occur at this next level of patterning. In the first phase, the d and d^{-1} processes were those which occurred between the Deep Structure and the Surface

Structure; here, in phase 2, the d and d^{-1} processes are operating between the Reference Structure and the Deep Structure.

The client's response to the Meta-model challenges to modal operators will be one of the forms of semantic ill-formedness. Minimally, since the therapist's challenge presupposes a semantically ill-formed Cause-Effect relation, the client's response will be ill formed in that specific way. In addition, the client may respond with the other forms of semantic ill-formedness:

Mind Reading
I know that my father would feel bad if I left home.
Lost Performative
It would be wrong to leave home.

The Meta-model challenge to Mind Reading is the v^{-1} challenge at this level of structure:

Therapist: How, specifically, do you know that your father . . . ?

The Meta-model challenge to the lost performative is the d^{-1} challenge at the first level of patterning — a deletion inverse which applies between Deep and Surface Structure (as, in fact, the linguistic representation of performative deletion is a Deep Structure to Surface Structure process). If the client responds with a Cause-Effect statement such as:

My father's feeling bad stops me from leaving home.

then, the usual Meta-model challenge v^{-1} applies, requesting that the client specify the process by which this claimed causal connection occurs.

More important for understanding the overall strategy, however, is the fact that the two major forms of semantic ill-formedness, Cause-Effect and Mind-Reading, are the linguistic representations of fuzzy functions over which the client is, at present, exercising no control. Thus, the emergence of modal operators and the successful applications of the d^{-1}, r^{-1}, v^{-1} and n^{-1} processes at level 1 (between Deep Structure and Surface Structure) and at level 2 (between Reference Structure and Deep Structure) signal the therapist that it is time to move into the third phase — that of selecting the technique for assisting the client in changing.

SELECTING THE TECHNIQUE FOR CHANGE

Here the therapist is ready to select a technique for assisting the client in changing. In the first two phases, he has identified the portions of the client's model which are impoverished and then the limits of the client's model. In challenging these limits, the therapist receives from the client the identification of the major semantically ill-formed modeling process involved in the client's organization of this portion of his model. The selection and implementation of an effective technique for change will be the therapist's major task in this phase. In order to make a good selection, the therapist can construct and evaluate what we call the *instantaneous description* of the client. By an instantaneous description, we mean a representation of the client which gives the minimal amount of information sufficient to allow the therapist to select and implement an effective technique for change. In our experience, we have evolved a six-tuple — a vector which has six positions for information. Each of these six positions or variables has various possible values called the range of the variable. The complete vector consists of the instantaneous description of the client and includes information sufficient for the selection and employment of a change technique. We represent the vector as:

$$< I, R, O, S, F, M >$$

where:

I   is a variable covering the input channel which the client is using for this problem;

R   is a variable covering the client's Most Highly Valued Representational System for this problem;

O   is a variable covering the Output Channel which the client is using for this problem;

S   is a variable covering the client's Satir Category under stress for this problem;

F   is a variable covering the type of Semantic Ill-Formedness which the client is using for this problem;

M   is the most frequently occurring violation of the Meta-model distinctions for this problem.

We now list the six variables and their associated ranges:

I = { V (visual), K (kinesthetic), A (auditory), D (digital) }
R = { V (visual), K (kinesthetic), A (auditory), D (digital) }

$$O = \{ \text{V (visual), K (kinesthetic), A (auditory), D (digital)} \}$$
$$S = \left\{ \begin{array}{l} \text{1 (placating), 2 (blaming), 3 (super-reasonable),} \\ \text{4 (irrelevant)} \end{array} \right\}$$
$$F = \left\{ \begin{array}{l} \text{CE (cause-effect), MR (mind reading),} \\ \text{LP (lost performative)} \end{array} \right\}$$
$$M = \left\{ \begin{array}{l} \text{d (deletion), v (unspecified verb), r (lack of} \\ \text{referential index), n (nominalization)} \end{array} \right\}$$

For example, consider the following:

Michael is telling his therapist about his inability to cope with assignments at college. He begins by stating in a whining tone of voice that he "feels crushed by the amount of work." And school is destroying his sense of confidence. "I tried complaining to my professors about the inadequacy of the educational system, but they only patronize me. And I feel even worse when I'm trying to explain to them and their expression of being sorry for me — I just get sick to my stomach."

As Michael presented his story, his body was gesturing by pointing his finger as if scolding a child and his hand was pounding on the arm of the chair.

An instantaneous description of Michael could be taken by the following process:

	Primary		
$I = V$	Input	Visual	He saw amount of work and expression of sorrow.
$R = K$	Represen-tational system	Kinesthetic	Felt crushed, feel even worse, sick to stomach.
$S = 2$	Satir category	Blaming	Pointing finger, harsh tone, complaining to professors. Referential index of responsibility.
$F = CE$	Semantic ill-formedness	Cause-Effect	Work makes him feel crushed. Professors make him feel sick. School is destroying his self-confidence.
$M = N$	Meta-model violation	Nominalization	School, sense of confidence. Inadequacy of educational system. Expression of sorrow.
$O = D$	Output channel	Digital	Complains as he talks.

So the resulting primary equation or instantaneous description would be represented as:

$$\text{Michael} \quad - \quad (V, K, D, 2, CE, n)$$

when the general form of the vector is

$$(I, R, O, S, F, M)$$

Now the question arises of how this representation can be a useful skill and tool for the therapist. Better stated, what set of conditions would permit a therapist to formulate a strategy for effective therapy devoid of content? This brings us to the concept of *Next-Step Function*. A next-step function would be the appropriate strategy for therapy, or the set of conditions which would indicate the needed technique for some well-formed outcome in therapy. Once again, the notion of well-formedness becomes an invaluable tool.

As you will recall, we stated in Parts II and III that well-formed sorting of polarities is required for integration to take place and for growth and coping to occur. Also, you will remember that, in the section on fuzzy functions, ill-formed equations resulted in a lack of choice and thus inadequate coping. Michael's equation (instantaneous description) from above is not well formed. Visual information is being represented kinesthetically — a fuzzy function which is causing him pain and blocking him from getting the things he wants from life. In order to construct a strategy for therapy based on his description, we must first map out the well-formedness constraints.

WELL-FORMEDNESS CONSTRAINTS FOR THERAPY

The following section will present the formal constraints for well-formed therapy; however, it is not our intention in this volume to be either exhaustive or complex. We understand that most therapists do not have an extensive background in advanced logic or group theory, so the following will remain at a low level of complexity representing only the most necessary, essential patterns for effective therapy. Although this will result in only the simplest formal notational system for therapy, we believe it best serves the purpose of providing serious clinicians with a viable tool at a level they will be able both to understand and to utilize as a tool for simultaneous diagnosis and treatment of the clients whom they are assisting to have more choices about their lives.

To build a viable formal notational system for therapy, we must, of course, as we did in the section on Fuzzy Functions, be able to notate incongruities and polarities. So we can add now to our system *double entries*, one representing each set of para-messages.

instantaneous description A (I, R, O, S, F, M)
instantaneous description B (I, R, O, S, F, M)

This will allow us to build two levels of constraints for well-formed therapy. First, the relationship between the members of one set, and, second, the relationship between sets of instantaneous descriptions. What follows are two sets of necessary well-formedness conditions for a well-formed instantaneous description in therapy. Once these have been established, we can proceed to construct the rules of derivation that will transform ill-formed descriptions into well-formed descriptions. This will not only give us explicit strategies for therapy but also a viable way of knowing when we have accomplished the task of therapy and when change has occurred. The therapist who uses this tool will at last be freed from the nagging question of knowing when he is finished, or if he has accomplished anything, which, in our experience, is the plight of most of the therapists we meet.

1. An instantaneous description will be well formed when:

$$(I_i, R_j, \_, \_, \_, \_)$$

where $i = j$

(that is, when the system the person uses to represent his experience is the one most naturally associated with the input channel through which he received the information, e.g., as input and as representational system)

and will be considered ill-formed when:

$$(I_i, R_j, \_, \_, \_, \_)$$

where $i \neq j$

Essentially, this condition states that fuzzy functions will not be considered well formed. Specifically, for example, any description in which visual information is simultaneously represented kinesthetically is not a well-formed description.

The simultaneous descriptions in the left-hand column are ill formed while those in the right-hand column are well formed.

$$(V, K, —, —, —, —) \qquad (V, V, —, —, —, —)$$
$$(A, K, —, —, —, —) \qquad (A, A, —, —, —, —)$$
$$(A, V, —, —, —, —) \qquad (K, K, —, —, —, —)$$
$$(K, A, —, —, —, —) \qquad (D, D, —, —, —, —)$$

2. An instantaneous description will be well formed when:

$$(—, R_i, —, S_j, —, —)$$

where i and j have the following **paired** values:

i	j
K	1
V	2
A	3

All other paired values will be considered ill formed in therapy.

3. An instantaneous description will be well formed when:

$$(—, —, O_i, S_j, —, —)$$

where paired values of i and j are **not** one of the following:

i	j
K	2
K	3

Note that all other relationships are not necessarily well formed — they can be ill formed in relation to values of other variables in the six-tuple vector. For example, the paired values for the S and O variables given by the instantaneous description,

$$(—, —, K, 1, —, —)$$

are well formed by our well-formedness condition 3. However, when the value of the M parameter is n, the instantaneous description is ill formed. In other words, while the pair K 1 is well formed for the parameters O and S, the triplet,

$$(\_, \_, K, 1, \_, n)$$

is ill formed. We are aware that the three well-formedness conditions presented above are not exhaustive for the well-formedness conditions for six tuples. We offer them as an example of the way in which a full model of the set of well-formed, instantaneous descriptions can be developed.

WELL-FORMEDNESS CONDITIONS FOR PAIRS OF INSTANTANEOUS DESCRIPTIONS

We present two examples of the translation of techniques presented in this volume into the formal notation to show the way in which the six-tuple can be used to assist you, as a therapist, in organizing your experiences in your work. Sets of simultaneous descriptions are of value in working with incongruities in a single individual and in the context of family therapy. In the first case — that of individual therapy — the six-tuple provides a way of defining the notions of congruity and incongruity. We define a function, Q, over the set of values occurring in the parameter O such that,

$$Q\ (O_i) = \text{meaning of the message carried by the output channel } O_i$$

Given the function Q and an instantaneous description, incongruity can be defined as the case in which there is more than one entry for the value of the O parameter, such that,

$$Q\ (O_i) \ne Q\ (O_j)$$

(where $\ne$ means *is not consistent with*)

for the same individual. In other words, given a six-tuple representation for the same individual,

$$\left(\_, \_, \left\{ \begin{matrix} O_i \\ O_j \end{matrix} \right\}, \_, \_, \_ \right)_{c^1}$$

where $Q\ (O_i) \ne Q\ (O_j)$

or, equivalently,

$$(\underline{\quad}, \underline{\quad}, O_i, \underline{\quad}, \underline{\quad}, \underline{\quad})_{c^1}$$

and

$$(\underline{\quad}, \underline{\quad}, O_j, \underline{\quad}, \underline{\quad}, \underline{\quad})_{c^1}$$

where $Q(O_i) \neq Q(O_j)$

the individual identified as c^1 is incongruent. If O_i and O_j are presented at the same time, then the six-tuple representations above identify a simultaneous incongruity — the case discussed in detail in the first portion of Part II. The client is presenting more than one message, and they do not match or fit together. If the above six-tuple representations are of the same client at two different points in a therapeutic session, then they represent sequential incongruity. For example, in the second phase of incongruity work, the client will have a set of instantaneous descriptions which meet the condition given below:

$$Q(O_i) \neq Q(O_j)$$
$$\text{for all i and j}$$

Congruency, in the language of the six-tuple, is the condition which occurs when:

$$Q(O_i) = Q(O_j) = , \ldots , = Q(O_k) = , \ldots , = Q(O_n)$$

for the same client at the same point in time.

We can generalize this process to other parameters and present a formal description of the point at which the therapist can know that Phase II of the incongruency work is finished and he may move with confidence to Phase III, integration.

A pair (set) of instantaneous descriptions will be well-formed with respect to the completion of Phase II of incongruency work when each six-tuple meets the well-formedness conditions specified above and,

$$(\underline{\quad}, R_i, O_j, S_k, \underline{\quad}, \underline{\quad})_{c^1}$$
$$(\underline{\quad}, R_i', O_j', S_k', \underline{\quad}, \underline{\quad})_{c^1}$$

where

$$R_i \neq R_i'$$

and

$$Q(O_j) \neq Q(O_j')$$

and

$$S_k \neq S_{k'}$$
for all i, j and k

This well-formedness condition shows that Phase II of incongruency work is complete when there is a maximal separation of the representational systems, output messages, and Satir categories.

As a second example, we present the technique of playing polarity. Suppose the therapist notices that the client is presenting incongruent messages — that is, suppose the client presents the therapist with the instantaneous description,

$$\left(\underline{\quad}, \text{v}, \begin{Bmatrix} O_j \\ O_k \end{Bmatrix}, 2, \underline{\quad}, \underline{\quad}\right)$$

where $Q(O_j) \neq Q(O_k)$

Suppose, further, that the therapist determines that $Q(O_j)$ is consistent with V as a value for the representational system variable, and that $Q(O_k)$ would be consistent with K and 1 as the values for the R and S variables. The therapist now decides to play polarity as described in Part II of this volume. Essentially, in the formal notation we are developing here, the therapist arranges his own instantaneous description to be more forceful than the instantaneous description presented by the client. In this particular case, he has two choices:

$$(\underline{\quad}, K, O_k, 1, \underline{\quad}, \underline{\quad})$$

or

$$(\underline{\quad}, V, O_j, 2, \underline{\quad}, \underline{\quad})$$

Since the client is already presenting the therapist with an instantaneous description which is closer to the second instantaneous description presented above, the therapist is interested in learning about the specific ways in which the client will present the less dominant polarity. Therefore, the therapist chooses to play the client's more dominant polarity, insuring that the client will flip polarities. Thus, the therapist arranges himself to present the client with the experience of:

$$(\underline{\quad}, V, O_j, 2, \underline{\quad}, \underline{\quad})$$

The client, responding to the shift in the therapist, will then change to the less dominant polarity, based on the Q (O_k) message. The therapist then has an understanding of the client's two polarities with which to work with him to make the changes he wants and needs for himself.

As a second example, consider the usefulness of the six-tuple approach to family therapy. One of the important checks which the therapist will make in the context of working with a family is to insure that the family members are able to exchange messages of appreciation (feedback) for one another. In the terminology we are developing here, the therapist is working to insure that the family members have a set of instantaneous descriptions which will have overlaps between the input and output channels of the family members sufficient to allow them to send and receive those messages of appreciation (feedback). Thus, one way that the therapist can use the six-tuple approach is to evaluate the well-formedness of the entire family system. For example, the following set of instantaneous descriptions identifies a family system in which communication between members 2 and 4 is not possible — an ill-formed set of instantaneous descriptions with respect to family communication possibilities:

$$(V, V, D, \_, \_, \_)_{c^1}$$
$$(K, K, D, \_, \_, \_)_{c^2}$$
$$(A, K, K, \_, \_, \_)_{c^3}$$
$$(V, K, D, \_, \_, \_)_{c^4}$$

Notice that, in this family system, the family member c^3 is the pivot member with respect to communication. Each of the other family members has a digital (D) output system as primary (language) and, furthermore, since family member c^3 has kinesthetic (K) as his primary output system, he can communicate with family member c^2 kinesthetically (touching, for example) and with both family members c^1 and c^4 by body movements (a K output system for c^3), since both of them have the ability to see those body messages. (They both have a visual input system as primary.)

NEXT-STATE FUNCTIONS

As we mentioned in the beginning of this part, the most general representation for the process of change which occurs in therapy using functional notation is:

therapist (client state$_i$)——————————————→(client state$_j$)

While this representation is accurate, it is of no value to us as practitioners of the art of therapy and change as it is too general to be of value in organizing and guiding our behavior in the therapeutic context. As we have continuously emphasized with concepts such as models of the world and the dangers which accompany the Lost Performative, the value of any representation (mathematical, verbal, etc.) must be relativized to its use. The question which we have found of value in our work is not whether the models we have constructed are true or accurate but, rather, whether they are useful in our work of assisting clients to gain more choices in the areas of their behavior in which they desire more options, and, simultaneously, of course, will result in a gain of more choices for us as effective, dynamic therapists.

Furthermore, as we stated previously, to employ the functional notation in a way that is useful requires that we are able to identify:

(1) The sets of experiences being associated (the domain and range);
(2) The regularities in the way these sets are associated (the function, rule of correspondence or rule of association connecting the sets).

One of the most useful concepts which we have adopted in our work comes from an area of mathematics known as Automata Theory, the theory of abstract machines. This branch of mathematics is closely connected with modern linguistic theory. Noam Chomsky, for example, the founder of modern transformational linguistics, developed several of the proofs basic to the field of automata theory. The concept which we wish to introduce is implicit in what we have already presented in this part — the notion called the *next-state function*. Essentially, the next-state function is another way of describing a function. Stated simply, given a certain state of the world and an action, some other state of the world will result. As with the functional notation which we have already introduced, the next-state function notation requires only that we be able to identify:

(a) A set of variables which adequately describe for the purposes for which we wish to use the model the initial state of the world (or the portion of the world we are interested in modeling) — the domain of the function —

184 / PART V

and a set of variables which adequately describe the set of possible resultant states of the world — the range of the function.

(b) A set of variables which adequately describe the set of acts which we are interested in understanding and of which we are building a model — the function or rule of association connecting the sets.

The six-tuple which we have developed in our work is a first approximation to a set of variables which will serve as the basis for an adequate description of a formal model for therapeutic change. Fortunately, this same set of variables serves as an adequate descriptive vocabulary for both the domain and the range of the next-state functions which we have found effective in our therapeutic work and in our work of constructing explicit models of the powerful therapeutic maneuvers of well-known therapists such as Virginia Satir and Milton H. Erickson (see *Patterns of the Hypnotic Techniques of Milton H. Erickson, M. D.,* Bandler and Grinder, Meta Productions, 1975). As we specified when we introduced the notion of instantaneous description, each of the six variables has a small number of possible values. Since the number of possible values is small, the six-tuple has worked as a highly efficient and powerful model, both in our own therapy and in our teaching in our Therapist Training Seminars. It has allowed people training to be therapists to organize their experience in the complex environment of ongoing face-to-face therapy with clients in such a way as to allow them to assist their clients in rapid, lasting, and satisfying change. Now, using the functional notation we have offered, we can refine the maximally general representation of change in therapy given previously to:

$$f\,(I, R, O, S, I\text{-}F, M)_c \longrightarrow (I, R, O, S, I\text{-}F, M)_c$$

where the variables of the six-tuples listed have the full possible range of values specified previously,

and

f is the next-state function

and

the subscript c identifies the six-tuple as the client's instantaneous description

The model which we have presented, then, makes the claim that the art of therapeutic change involves human changes which can be described adequately with the vocabulary of the six-tuple.

The set of six-tuples which may occur in the range of the function *f* are a proper subset of the set of all logically possible combinations of the values of the variables of the six-tuple. In other words, the outcome of the therapeutic encounter is restricted to certain vectors or instantaneous descriptions of the client. This is one way of capturing the belief that, in therapy, not every change is considered a successful outcome; rather, only certain kinds of change. The specific way in which we have developed restrictions on the set of all possible instantaneous descriptions to identify those which are acceptable outcomes (or next-states) for therapy is the use of well-formedness conditions of the six-tuple. For example, the following instantaneous description of a client after therapy is not acceptable or well formed in our model:

$$(\_, \_, K, 2, \_, \_)$$

In other words, a client whose instantaneous description identifies him as a blamer with a kinesthetic output system is not a well-formed outcome for therapy in our model. Thus, the model we present, specifically, the range of the function, can be further specified:

$$f \, (I, R, O, S, I\text{-}F, M) \longrightarrow (Y)$$

where Y is the set of acceptable six-tuples as specified by the well-formedness conditions for instantaneous descriptions

Next, consider the domain of the function. In traditional medical and psychotherapeutic models, the domain of the therapeutic function is the set of syndromes, the patterns of symptoms, or the basis of diagnosis. If diagnosis has any value in therapy, it is only so in that it identifies commonly occurring instantaneous descriptions of clients seeking therapeutic assistance *and at the same time* specifies a set of appropriate and effective maneuvers or interventions on the part of the therapist or doctor. It is with both of these criteria in mind that we constructed the present model. At present, we have not restricted the domain of the function in any way — there are no logical possibilities in the set of all six-tuples of which we are aware which could not occur. As we indicated in various parts of this volume, there are frequently occurring, ill-formed six-tuples. For example, one of the most common ill-formed combinations is:

$$(I_i, R_j, —, —, C\text{-}E, —)$$

where $i \neq j$ (that is, where the client whose six-tuple this is has a fuzzy function — he represents his experience from one input channel in a non-associated representational system)

The Meta-Tactic which we indicated is that of assisting the client in breaking the fuzzy function to give him the choice of:

$$(I_i, R_j, —, —, —, —)$$

where $i = j$

or the fuzzy function represented above.

Notice that, with this last discussion, we have begun the process of specifying the set of therapeutic functions — the class represented in our notation by the symbol f. The complete specification of f would be a formalization of the set of effective therapeutic maneuvers or interventions for acceptable therapeutic change. Employing the concept of next-state function,

f is the set of all functions such that

$$f(X) \longrightarrow (Y)$$

where X is the set of all possible six-tuples and Y is the set of well-formed six-tuples.

In words, f is any therapeutic intervention, any action on the part of the therapist, which results in a next-state, instantaneous description which meets the well-formedness conditions for six-tuples. The Meta-model challenges we have developed in Volume I of the *Magic* series are an explicit and adequate set of therapeutic interventions at the *verbal* level. These challenges specify for the set of all possible *verbal* productions by the client (the client's Surface Structures) the appropriate *verbal* intervention by the therapist. These *verbal* interventions are purely formal — independent of content. At the level of structure of the six-tuple, the Meta-Tactics which we have developed function in the same capacity as the Meta-model challenges do at the verbal level of structure. Consider, for example, the set of Meta-Tactics for working with the client who displays incongruity in his communication. Suppose that the client has an instantaneous description such as:

$$(—, K, — 2, —, —)_c$$

The therapist's task is to sort this simultaneous incongruity into a sequential incongruity — in other words to convert the above six-tuple into a pair of six-tuples, each of which is well formed,

$$f(\_\_, K, \_\_, 2, \_\_, \_\_)_c \longrightarrow \left\{ \begin{array}{l} (\_\_, V, \_\_, 2, \_\_, \_\_) \\ (\_\_, K, \_\_, 1, \_\_, \_\_) \end{array} \right\}$$

In the terms stated in the portion of the book on incongruity work, the therapist must sort the paramessages into two congruent polarities. We listed there a number of Meta-Tactics for achieving a well-formed sort. Take the Meta-Tactic 1 — movie/play director. Here the therapist uses verbal instructions and kinesthetic instructions (molding the client's body into a more congruent posture). In this case, the value of f is the set of verbal and kinesthetic inputs from the therapist to the client. Another way in which the therapist can maneuver is to use the technique of playing polarities (presented in the incongruity chapter). Faced with the six-tuple above, the therapist might choose to arrange all his output channels in a way which is more forceful than one of the polarities partially displayed by the client in the six-tuple above. For example, the therapist may choose to present the client with the following six-tuple:

$$(\_\_, V, \_\_, 2, \_\_, \_\_)_t \quad \text{where } t = \text{therapist}$$

The result of the therapist's playing polarity in this specific way will be for the client to flip to the other polarity represented partially in the original six-tuple:

$$(\_\_, K, \_\_, 1, \_\_, \_\_)_c$$

In the next state function notation which we have presented, then, this entire portion of the therapeutic encounter in which the therapist identifies and sorts the client's incongruent paramessages can be represented as:

$$(\_\_, V, \_\_, 2, \_\_, \_\_)_t \left[(\_\_, K, \_\_, 2, \_\_, \_\_)_c \right] \longrightarrow (\_\_, K, \_\_, 1, \_\_, \_\_)_c$$

This translation of one of the therapist's techniques into the formal notation demonstrates one important feature — namely, that an adequate vocabulary for describing the set of therapeutic intervention, the set f, will include the same vocabulary which serves as the vocabulary for the domain and range of the set of functions f.

A complete formalization of therapy would identify for each member of the set of logically possible six-tuples (that is, the domain of the function), a set of maneuvers or interventions (the set f) and the specific outcome or client's next-state (restricted to the set of well-formed-in-therapy six-tuples) which are the result of the operation of each of the members of f specified as appropriate for the initial state the client presented. The complete formalization of therapeutic change is the research domain for the ongoing activity of people-helpers. The actual experience of working with the process of change in the context of people in therapy must lead into this area if the resulting formalized model is to be useful. Our purpose in this portion of *Magic II* has been to establish a notational system with a vocabulary adequate to assist therapists in organizing and communicating their experience in a way which will immediately allow them to improve their skills as people-helpers and, ultimately, to develop a full, formal model of change adequate to meet the needs of the people who come to us for help. In the following section, we present an example of effective therapeutic change in which the therapist employs several of the Meta-Tactics which we presented previously with parallel formalization of the therapeutic encounter, using the formal notational system we have presented here. We hope that this will serve as a guide and a first step in establishing the complete formal model for therapeutic change.

ILLUSTRATION OF A FORMAL NOTATION AS A TOOL FOR THERAPY

The following is a formal representation of a portion of a complete therapeutic session for the purpose of assisting you in adapting this system in your own work, whether clinical, research or theoretical. The purpose here is to demonstrate how this formal notation can serve as a diagnostic tool at the same time that it provides a strategy for the clinician to guide his behavior in therapy, assisting the clinician from whatever school of therapy in developing an effective plan to assist his clients in changing in a way which results in the desired choices for the client.

Tom has been referred by his probation officer for therapy. He is a "juvenile delinquent" who is serving time in an institution for beating up his sister and generally anyone else he gets the chance to. Strangely enough, he is quite remorseful over his actions, but he continues to steal and fight and then apologizes. He was presented to the authors as one of those "you can't do it" cases by friends who are clinicians and seem very much to enjoy testing the authors at every chance. However, this also appeared to us to be an excellent opportunity to demonstrate to our friends the value of formal notation (something they scoffed at) and, at the same time, help Tom, if we could. We consulted Tom to find out if he was willing to participate in our demonstration. He agreed and even seemed quite genuine in his desire to overcome his "problems." The session began with Tom telling the authors what he believed he needed to change about himself. We wrote an instantaneous description on the blackboard as he spoke.

1. $(V, K, D, 2, CE, \_)_c$

After identifying the ill-formed description, one of the authors commented to the watching clinicians about the R and S variables with values K and 2, respectively, and the variables I and R with values V and K, respectively, describing choices of applying the inverse function of Meta-model questions or the development of new representational systems. Then the other choice, the next-step function tactic called playing polarity, was done by that author adopting part of Tom's description and applying it as a next-step function with Tom.

2. $(\_, \_, D_v, 2, \_, \_)_t \; [(V, K, D, 2, CE, \_)_c]$
    where D_v identifies the language output of the therapist using visual predicates

The result was a change in his description to:

3. $(V, K, D, 1, MR, V)_c$

Now having two instantaneous descriptions, the authors explained how choices could be based on the two descriptions, either building new representational systems directly or applying Meta-model inverse functions. A double bind could be constructed. Many choices were available, but the most obvious was to sort the sets of vectors into polarities, using any of the techniques for that purpose provided in this volume. We chose to use spatial sorting of polarities, as kinesthetic was his most highly valued representational system and would be the easiest technique to use with him. Two chairs were placed facing each other, in Gestalt fashion, using spatial locations and the sorting principles of Satir category and representational system predicates as gauges of a well-formed sort of paramessages and maximal separation.

The resulting sort was two sequentially expressed polarities:

$$(V, V, D_i, 2, CE, \_)$$

and

$$(V, K, D_j, 1, MR, \_)$$
$$\text{where } Q(D_i) \neq Q(D_j)$$

Having sorted the polarities into a well-formed split, the authors explained the number of choices available to him to move into the third phase of polarity work, integration. Both polarities must now be mapped into the same representational system; this, of course, can be done in a number of ways and in a number of systems. A next-state function that must be applied to achieve this mapping, however, has the same formal characteristics, no matter what technique is employed. The formal notation of this function itself suggests a number of approaches; for example, since:

$$(\_, V, \_, \_, \_, \_)$$

and

$$(\_, K, \_, \_, \_, \_)$$

we might select the unused representational system for Phase 3. At this time, the authors paused to review the process which had occurred and to give the observers some strategies to decide what the best technique was for mapping polarities into contact and the client into meta-position. Basically, we reasoned that, since Tom's most highly valued representational system is kinesthetic (K) and his ability to access visually is poorly developed as a representational system, mapping into V would be difficult. Mapping into K would be easy; however, the choice of another representational system would develop a new way of representing his experience for Tom. We understand that, unless an input channel is totally closed, the information arriving through that channel is represented in the associated representational system — even though it may have no relationship to the polarities and coping with which we are working directly. Since the most well-formed function in therapy is the one which results in a congruent, instantaneous description or vector, we proposed to try what might be called complex integration (integration which does more than just solve one ill-formed coping pattern — one which opens many channels to growth and potential for the client). Our strategy for this is a simple one: to map Tom's polarities simultaneously into K through D and A, resulting in simultaneous representation — that is, meta-position. Simultaneous representation in K can be quite uncomfortable, as you may have noticed if you have ever watched and listened in therapy to a couple argue, when you were, yourself, either see-feeling or hear-feeling. For the purpose of a dramatic demonstration (the authors being showmen at heart and realizing that dramatic demonstrations motivate clinicians to undergo the struggle of learning new techniques and ways of approaching therapy), we chose for each of the authors to play one of Tom's polarities as if we were that part of him. And to do it simultaneously and more forcefully than he could. We explained calmly to him as follows:

> *Therapist:* Tom, you understand that there are two parts of yourself, one in that chair who gets angry and yells. He wants you to stand up for yourself and not get pushed around. He sees things happen he doesn't like and tells you you should beat up people, and not be a sissy, is that right?

> *Tom:* Yes.

> *Therapist:* And you have another part, over there, who is afraid sometimes and feels it is wrong to hurt people, or to say mean things to them and hurt their feelings. He tells you to apologize and to be a good guy so people will like you, is that right?

> *Tom:* Yes. I have both of them, and they fight with each other just like what I have been doing in these two chairs, only in my head until I blow up. Then I do the wrong thing and get in trouble again. And all along I know better and everybody tells me I know better, but I just sort of lose control of this one (points to chair of blaming polarity) and whamo! Then that one (points to placating chair) comes along and tells me to apologize, calls me names (notice predicate shift), and everybody thinks I'm crazy.

> *Therapist:* You're not crazy and I think we can get you through this if you will stick it out through something that might be a little unusual and maybe a little scary. John is going to play the part of you which gets angry, that one over there, and I'm going to play the part of you which tells you to apologize and be a good boy, that one over there. Will you play with us and promise to stay with it to the end?

> *Tom:* Sure, if you think it will help

> *Therapist:* Good.

Both the authors immediately and abruptly, taking Tom by surprise, began to argue with each other, just as Tom had done when his polarities were first spatially and then maximally sorted into a well-formed pair of vectors.

$$\left\{ \begin{array}{l} (\underline{\quad}, \underline{\quad}, D_v, 2, CE, v)\,\text{John} \\[2mm] (\underline{\quad}, \underline{\quad}, D_k, 1, MR, v)\,\text{Richard} \end{array} \right\} \longrightarrow \text{Tom}$$

The authors exaggerated this process, each demanding simultaneously that Tom listen to him, accede to his demands, and ignore the other author.

Essentially, this put Tom in the meta-position of receiving both of his own polarities simultaneously in each of his input and associated representational systems.

$$\left\{ \begin{array}{l} Q\,(O_i)\,\text{John} \\[2mm] Q\,(O_j)\,\text{Richard} \end{array} \right\} \longrightarrow \text{as input to Tom}$$

where $i \neq j$

Contact and meta-position have now been achieved, the resulting message response — output channel — was pure auditory: a scream and a digital "shut up." Final recoding and integration were the next step.

The authors now persistently demanded that Tom take control of them as his parts, or they would resume the simultaneous playing of his two polarities, demanding that he listen to each and mediate from a position of control between the two, recognizing the resources of each verbally, and then himself building a viable structure in which each part would have freedom to be expressed, acknowledging the need to use both for balance.

Tom thereby recoded his parts from the *source* of his troubles to *resources* to cope with the task of living. After verbally recoding each part, integration was achieved in his kinesthetic system, having him take from each author the defined abilities, one in each hand, and delicately weaving them together and spreading them throughout his whole self (body, eyes, etc.). Recoding, of course, does not really occur outside in the client's hands, but the kinesthetic act is accompanied by neurologically constructing a new map for the territory where previously there had been two conflicting maps. The resulting vectors were a set of instantaneous directions; Tom's choices:

$$(V, V, D_v, 2, CE, \_)_c$$
$$(K, K, K, 1, MR, \_)_c$$
$$(A, D, D, \_, \_, \_)_c$$

Although this is not a totally well-formed, instantaneous description, the changes in Tom were substantial for one session, and these changes were apparent to those around him. This session served as an adequate example of how a formal notation system helps both to clarify what happens in the process of therapy and to serve as a guide for clinicians to design their own techniques and strategies for assisting their clients in the process of change.

Epilogue

In the two volumes of *The Structure of Magic*, we have tried in the best way we know how to show some of the many patterns that therapists of every school have in common. We never had the intention of starting a new *school* of therapy; we wished, rather, to start a new way of *talking* about therapy so that the similarities of different schools approaching the task of helping people to change could be understood. We wished to demonstrate, not that any particular approach to therapy is any more potent than any other approach, but that all forms of therapy assist their clients in changing. So the question is no longer which approach is the best; it is how such seemingly different approaches all can work.

The answer we presented in these first two volumes is basically a simple one. All the techniques of every form of therapy are techniques which affect the processes of representation, the creation and organization of a client's model of the world. To the degree that techniques induce change in a client's modeling of the world is the degree to which they will be effective in assisting a client to change. As a client's model of the world changes, his perceptions change and so, too, does his behavior. The processes by which a person's model of the world becomes impoverished are the same processes by which it can be enriched — the processes of Deletion, Distortion, and Generalization. All forms of therapy, all the techniques of the different forms of therapy — in fact, all learning — can be understood in terms of the processes of representation.

We have always found it uncanny that the techniques of

therapy mirror so precisely the disorders of the mind found in the chronic wards of mental hospitals. Techniques of age regression; techniques of disassociation, such as the sorting techniques presented in Part II of this volume; the Gestalt techniques; the projective techniques of art therapy ... the list goes on and on, permutations of every form of therapy. We, as therapists, in essence use the formal patterns present in psychotic and schizophrenic behavior to assist our clients in growing and changing in ways which enrich their lives. This suggests that Ronald Laing is right when he describes schizophrenia as a natural process of change. The therapist's role is more that of a guide using the natural processes already at work in people all of the time. We have found in our experience that the behavior of schizophrenics and psychotics is highly repetitive — it is as if they are stuck in one pattern which they follow over and over again. We have often thought that they are living, perhaps, in a repetitive dream which must be dreamt again and again, seeking the resolution to some incomplete pattern.

We have also thought that these "mentally ill" people are simply an exaggerated example of the way most human beings live their lives, that perhaps they have been locked up — hidden from view — because they are a symbol of the repetitive, dried up, colorless lives which many "normal" human beings live. In some sense, this was the purpose of the human potential movement — to make psychology available to everyone, so that all of us could live happier and more creative lives. Fritz Perls once said, " .... Man lives in a state of low grade vitality. Though generally he does not suffer deeply, he also knows little of true creative living."

With this thought in mind, we ask you to think of *The Structure of Magic* as we do: we understand it to be not only a book for changing personality but, also, to be the first book on creative and generative personality.

Finally, we would like to remind the readers of the two volumes of *The Structure of Magic* that it is only a way of talking about it.

Bibliography

Altshuler and Comalli, in the *Journal of Auditory Research*, Washington, D.C.

Bach-y-Rita, P. *Brain Mechanisms in Sensory Substitution*. New York: Academic Press, 1972.

Bandler, R., and Grinder, J. *Patterns of the Hypnotic Techniques of Milton H. Erickson, M.D.* Cupertino, Calif.: Meta Publications, 1975.

Bandler, R., and Grinder, J. *The Structure of Magic I*. Palo Alto: Science and Behavior Books, 1975.

Bateson, G. *Steps to an Ecology of Mind*. New York: Ballantine Books, 1972.

Chomsky, N. *Aspects of the Theory of Syntax*. Cambridge, Mass.: MIT Press, 1965.

Chomsky, N. *Syntactic Structures*. The Hague: Mouton, 1957.

Dimond, S., and Beaumont, K. *Hemispheric Functions in the Human Brain*. New York: John Wiley & Sons, 1974.

Fagen, J. (ed.). *Gestalt Therapy Now*. Palo Alto: Science and Behavior Books, 1970.

Gazzaniga, M. *The Bisected Brain*. New York: Appleton, Century, & Croft, 1974.

Haley, J. (ed.). *Advanced Techniques of Hypnosis and Therapy: Selected Papers of Milton H. Erickson, M.D.* New York: Grune and Stratton, 1967.

Haley, J. *Strategies of Psychotherapy*. New York: Grune and Stratton, 1963.

Jackson, D. D. *Therapy, Communication and Change.* Palo Alto: Science and Behavior Books, 1968.

Korzybski, A. *Science and Sanity.* Lakeville, Connecticut: The International Non-Aristotelian Library Publishing Company, 4th Edition, 1933.

Laing, R. D. *The Politics of the Family and Other Essays.* London: Vintage Books, 1972.

Perls, F. *The Gestalt Approach: Eyewitness to Therapy.* Palo Alto: Science and Behavior Books, 1973.

Russell, B. *Introduction to Mathematical Philosophy.* London: George Allen and Unwin, Ltd., 2nd Edition, 1921.

Russell, B. *Principia Mathematica.* London: Cambridge University Press, 1910.

Satir, V. *Conjoint Family Therapy.* Palo Alto: Science and Behavior Books, 1964.

Satir, V. *Helping Families to Change.* Hays, Kansas: The High Plains Comprehensive Community Mental Health Center, 1972.

Satir, V. *Peoplemaking.* Palo Alto: Science and Behavior Books, 1972.

Schuchman, G., and Burgi, E. J., in the *Journal of Auditory Research,* Washington, D.C.

Watzlawick, P.; Weakland, J.; and Fisch, R. *Change.* New York: W. Norton, 1974.